AF422717

To my wife Oriana

Artificial intelligence for professions

An introduction for non-IT specialists

Roberto Magnani

Translation and update of
*"Intelligenza Artificiale per le professioni
edizione per non specialisti di informatica"*
EBS edition May 2023
Translation made by the author with the support of *ORSi Consilium* team

Dublin October 2024

Index

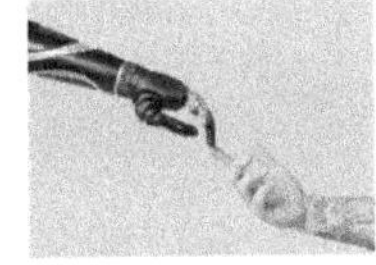

Annexes on glossary, terminology, Asilomar principles, EU Act

Introduction

The motivation for compiling a compendium of foundational Artificial Intelligence (AI) concepts raised from a series of discussions with professionals who, recognising the imminence of a transformative revolution, sought to be prepared without possessing specialised knowledge in computer science or mathematics. We are undoubtedly witnessing a paradigm shift, comparable to the epochal innovations of the wheel and writing, and more recently, the industrial revolution and the advent of the internet. This work is a response to the growing need for AI literacy and develop a comprehensive guide to AI fundamentals.

Readers' suggestions, following the essay's successful Italian publication, have driven the translation of the original text with some update.

As well known, historically, every revolution has originated a shift in power dynamics, leading to substantial societal changes that necessitate proactive preparation. In the specific context of Artificial Intelligence, the emergence of conversational services that engage in natural human interaction has ignited concerns and prompted numerous inquiries, particularly regarding their demonstrated capacity for autonomous learning.

It is noteworthy that AI-driven learning algorithms are already integrated into our daily lives, evident in our smartphones' facial recognition capabilities, photo classification functions, and not to mention "social" services that tailor recommendations to our preferences, proposing products and information aligned with our tastes. While these services have not garnered significant public attention to date, they are underpinned by AI-based learning and harbour real risks, both psychological, such as addiction, and social, including the potential to influence public opinion or manipulate individual habits

These risks have remained a bit under the radar until the moment when the ability to interact in a "human" and accessible way to the public has manifested itself, with the famous ChatGPT, or BARD and others. The falsifications of images and videos generated in a realistic way, but not related to real situations that have taken place, are known.

The clamour has therefore been activated more for an ancestral fear of the human being of meeting a more capable and therefore dangerous competitor. The apocalypse of humanity has always been one of the latent fears that we have carried with us for millennia. In the following chapters of the book, we will provide the elements to better understand where the risks are, providing some hints on how systems to Artificial Intelligence operate and some references to be able to adapt to the rapid change that is looming in all professions.

Artificial Intelligence is in fact bringing about a change in the various human activities. The presence and accessibility of data, now possible through the enhancement of the internet and communication techniques that allow exchanges between users that were impossible only a few years ago, is transforming virtually every aspect of the way we understand and model our world.

It must be said that the public has also contributed by sharing personal data with ease, which has allowed social and individual mappings that only in the nineties of the last century would have required costly dedicated surveys, sometimes impossible. This allows companies and organisations to handle large volumes of data that, analysed with the help of artificial intelligence, help to cover trends and models, helping to define market strategies and specific actions, commercial or social.

Questions that until recently were not even known to be able to ask can be asked. The automation of work flows and business processes can be improved more easily with almost immediate implementation, leading to a reduction in operating costs, or improving performance at the same time, obtaining better products.

But the applications are endless in all fields, as we will see. Finance, medicine, social sciences, law and legality, civil and architectural design, image management, art, etc., practically nothing escapes.

Next, we will go through the conceptual basics with some examples already in place in the main fields of human activity, without neglecting the ethical aspects and the risks that such a radical change necessarily brings with it.

The print English edition is a translation and update of the original book in Italian edited in 2023.

Milan/Dublin October 2024

Part One - The history and concepts

Chapter 1 - Classifications

There are many definitions of artificial intelligence, but for the moment we will stick to the most intuitive interpretation that defines artificial intelligence (AI) as a technology, or rather combinations of technologies, capable of imitating human intelligence. AI is based on the idea that a machine can be programmed to imitate and improve human abilities, such as perception, reasoning, judgment, and learning. In truth, there now exists a European law with a clear and very articulated definition of Artificial Intelligence. For a detailed analysis, we refer the reader to the text of the law reported at the bottom[1]

History

It all started in the summer of **1956, at a workshop at Dartmouth** College with scientists and mathematicians of the caliber of **Claude Shannon**, the father of information theory, **Marvin Minsky**, computer scientist and mathematician who founded the AI laboratory at MIT in Boston, **John McCarthy**, one of the leading founders and contributors to the development of robotics and **Nat Rochester,** IBM computer scientist, developer of the first assembler language. In general, it is considered that this was the occasion on which the concept of artificial intelligence was born with a visionary development plan. Scientists started from the assumption that every aspect of learning or any other characteristic of intelligence can be described in a mathematical, precise way, so that it can be simulated by a machine and create the conditions for designing neural networks capable of using language, forming abstractions, and improving themselves. At the time, they declared themselves convinced that the work of a summer would be enough to make significant progress. In reality, AI has gone through various phases of enthusiasm alternating with great disappointments for decades. The so called "winters for AI"

However, it should not be forgotten that the first great name linked to AI is certainly that of **Alan Turing**, who hypothesised the need to create specific

---

[1]EUR-Lex *https://eur-lex.europa.eu/eli/reg/2024/1689/oj, 2024*

algorithms to create **machines capable of learning,** and is considered by many to be the father of AI with the Turing machine, which provided a fundamental aid to solving World War II in favour of the Anglo-American forces. By **algorithm** he meant **a sequence of instructions/actions that must be executed in a specific order in a finite time.**

From the 1980s on, a series of interesting results has given new life to this area of research: a rebirth that has been made possible by new investments in the sector. It should be said that the original deterministic design proved impracticable and the evolution of **AI has passed through some shortcuts.** For example, **the use of statistics** because a deterministic structuring proved to be too complex and the use of data from the internet should also be considered a shortcut because by definition they are partial. However, as a result, at the end of the 1990s, machine learning found a new burst through a series of innovations in techniques linked to statistical and probabilistic elements, to end up being a well-recognised branch of research. By adopting statistical methods to simulate complex processes, we've introduced a shortcut that inherently comes with the risk of error, a common feature of such systems. (N. Cristianini *The shortcut,* 2023).

In fact the so called **"AI winters"** represent the cyclical nature of artificial intelligence research, marked by periods of intense hype and investment followed by disillusionment and a decline in interest. These cycles arise from the gap between the ambitious goals set for AI and the actual rate of progress.

And it still does not cease to excite and disappoint: as in the case of the enthusiasm for the eloquence of ChatGPT that gave way in a few months to a chorus of criticism for the errors that that form of AI does not cease to commit, to which are added the fears of an uncontrolled evolution of a non-human and hostile intelligence. The progress from the 1950s of the last century has been possible thanks to the advancement of technology that has allowed the generation and management of large amounts of data with the advent of communication techniques unthinkable only a few decades ago and that have contributed to a rapid acceleration of AI progress.

The **generative AI** has now entered a phase of **widespread diffusion in society**; in addition to the already mentioned ChatGPT for all of 2022 and the beginning of 2023, new large-scale AI models have been released every month. These models, ChatGPT, Stable Diffusion, Whisper and DALL-E, are capable of performing an increasingly wide range of tasks, from text manipulation and analysis, to image generation, to speech recognition. These systems demonstrate a question-answering ability and text, image, and code generation that were unthinkable ten years ago, and they surpass the state of the art on many benchmarks, old and new. However, they are exposed to misunderstandings or misinterpretations (that erroneously are called "hallucinations", referring to a mental disease that has nothing to do with an expectable error of a stochastic process), or with intrinsic biases that can induce critical and negative effects, whether intended or unintended, posing complicated ethical challenges. The political world is beginning to take note of this while the leaders of the sectors, private or public, who have already integrated AI in some way into their activities are finding tangible benefits in terms of economics and service efficiency.

It should be considered, however, that much still needs to be done to perfect a series of elements, algorithms, and technical structures. The future development possibilities of this branch are still to be discovered, the possible options are linked to virtually all scientific and technical sectors and are destined to introduce applications of great importance not only in the scientific and research field, but also, and it would be to say above all, in the social field and in everyday life.

Objectives of Artificial Intelligence

The **first** to define objectives and **rules** for AI was, in fact, a science fiction writer, **Isaac Asimov**, a hugely successful author, conceived the three laws of robotics, which, despite his reservations, became a fundamental reference point for AI development.

The benefit Asimov had in mind was the automation of repetitive, tedious, or dangerous tasks.

A **robot may not injure a human being** or, through inaction, allow a human being to come to harm.

A **robot must obey orders** given by human beings, except where such orders would conflict with the First Law.

A **robot must protect its own existence,** as long as such protection does not conflict with the First or Second Law.

We'll explore in the ethics chapter that these rules, while still valid, are no longer sufficient, and greater effort is required to ensure AI does no harm. From Asimov's original spirit, which sought in robots an aid for humans, one intention remains: **improving people's quality of life**. This is already happening in many fields, from daily assistance provided through internet-accessible functions to personalised healthcare or home care for the elderly, both in terms of monitoring and anticipating dangerous situations. Certainly, productivity and efficiency of processes are already improving, for example in finance or business in general, by analysing large amounts of data to identify patterns and trends. On this path, combined with advanced forms of computation given by supercomputers, or recently quantum computers, AI can be used to model and develop innovative material molecules or new drugs. Attempts to achieve autonomous vehicles or robots that can be used in domestic environments are in all the newspapers, while we've had operational robots in industrial fields for years.

Almost without realising it, **we're now accustomed** to examples of **AI in our daily lives**. Siri and Alexa are voice assistants that use AI to understand and respond to user requests. We experience product recommendations on Amazon and Netflix daily: AI is used to analyse users' purchase and viewing data to recommend products or programmes that might interest the user. Facial recognition allows identification of people in photos or videos, a fairly common use for public safety or event registration in various countries worldwide. Driverless underground trains are now widespread, with a demonstrated increase in safety and convenience for users.

Classification - Narrow AI

In literature, AI tends to be classified in three different ways, based on potential compared to human beings. Currently, the most widespread AI is classified as "weak or **narrow AI**". Indeed, many currently existing systems claiming to use "artificial intelligence" are operating as narrow AI, focused on specific tasks. This category includes the best-known existing applications such as industrial robots, Siri, Cortana, and Google Assistant, image/facial recognition software, disease mapping and prediction tools, anti-spam filters / social media monitoring tools for dangerous content, engagement or marketing tools that suggest listening or purchases based on internet behaviour.

Even if one might have the feeling that they act intelligently, these are machines that operate under a narrow set of constraints, hence the name weak or narrow AI. Narrow AI does not imitate or replicate human intelligence, but merely simulates human behaviour based on a narrow range of parameters and contexts. These systems can only learn or be trained to complete specific tasks.

Narrow AI has seen remarkable **growth** in the last decade, **fuelled by** advances in machine learning and neural networks, also called **deep learning**. Their usefulness lies in the ability to replicate human-like reasoning, but with the capacity to consider much more data at a much higher speed, constituting a valid aid, for example, to critical clinical decisions in healthcare.

It's primarily based on the use of natural language processing (NLP) to perform tasks. NLP is evident in "chatbots" (software that simulates and processes human conversations) and similar AI technologies. By understanding natural language speech and text, AI is programmed to interact with humans in a natural and personalised way. It can be reactive or have limited memory. Reactive AI is simple; it has no need for memory or data storage, emulating the human mind's ability to respond to different types of stimuli without considering previous experiences. Limited memory AI is more advanced, equipped with data memorisation and learning capabilities that allow machines to use historical data to make decisions. They typically handle large amounts of data, especially in the use of neural networks, which we'll explore in upcoming chapters. In the field of AI, systems are often categorised based on their capabilities compared to human intelligence. Currently, **the most prevalent form is known as "weak or narrow AI"** (also referred to as Narrow AI or ANI). This classification encompasses many of the AI systems we interact with daily, which excel at specific, well-defined tasks but lack the breadth of human cognitive abilities.

Machine learning, neural networks, and deep learning. These technologies have dramatically expanded the capabilities of AI systems, allowing them to tackle increasingly complex tasks with impressive efficiency. Just as summary of latest progresses systems like GPT-4, ChatGPT, and Google's PaLM have revolutionised natural language processing. These models can generate human-like text, translate languages, write different kinds of creative content, and answer questions in an informative way. They've found applications in customer service, content creation, and even coding assistance.

AI models such as DALL-E, Mid-journey, and Stable Diffusion have demonstrated the ability to create highly realistic images and artwork from text descriptions. This technology is reshaping fields like graphic design, advertising, and digital art.

While Siri, Alexa, and Google Assistant have been around for a while, they've become increasingly sophisticated. They can now handle complex queries, control smart home devices, and even engage in more natural, context-aware conversations.

Companies like Tesla, Waymo, and Cruise have made significant strides in. These systems use a combination of computer vision, sensor fusion, and decision-making algorithms to navigate complex road environments.

AI is making substantial impacts in medicine, from analysing medical images to predicting patient outcomes. For instance, DeepMind's AlphaFold has made groundbreaking progress in predicting protein structures, which could accelerate drug discovery and our understanding of diseases.

Robo-advisors and AI-driven trading algorithms have become more prevalent in the financial sector. These systems can analyse market trends, manage portfolios, and even detect fraudulent transactions with increasing accuracy.

AI tools are now assisting in various design fields. For example, Autodesk's generative design software can create optimised product designs based on specific constraints and goals. Beyond just controlling non-player characters,

AI is now being used to generate entire game worlds, create realistic character behaviours, and even adapt game difficulty in real-time based on player performance.

Despite these impressive capabilities, it's crucial to remember that these are all examples of narrow AI. Each system is designed and trained for a specific set of tasks and lacks the general problem-solving abilities of humans. They operate within predefined parameters and don't possess true understanding or consciousness.

As we look to the future, the boundaries of narrow AI continue to expand. Researchers are working on making these systems more robust, ethical, and capable of handling increasingly complex tasks. However, the leap from narrow AI to artificial general intelligence (AGI) remains a significant challenge that goes beyond simply improving existing systems.

Artificial General Intelligence - Strong AI

In its continuous and unstoppable progress, research in universities and large multinational companies is trying to reach a higher level of AI, what is called **general AI (AGI - Artificial General Intelligence)**, which some also call strong AI or deep artificial intelligence. This is the attempt to give a representation of human cognitive capabilities, generalised in software so that, faced with an unfamiliar task, the AGI system can find a solution in a given situation in a way indistinguishable from that of a human being.

It has not yet been achieved, although research is making considerable progress. To succeed, it's necessary to make machines aware, programming a complete set of cognitive abilities. Experience-based learning should develop to a higher level than we currently know, not only improving efficiency on single tasks, but acquiring the ability to apply experience to a wider range of different problems, in a totally autonomous way, and someone thinks that with the current logic based on Boolean logic it is not possible to recreate the conditions of awareness that should characterise a true general AI

In this area, progress must be borrowed from ongoing studies of the structure of the human mind. It's the only way to define how to induce the ability to discern needs and emotions and to recreate thought processes with human-like intelligence and self-aware consciousness capable of solving problems, learning, and making plans for the future. It is called Neuromorphic Computing: this approach aims to mimic the structure and function of the human brain in hardware. Projects like Intel's Loihi chip and IBM's TrueNorth are exploring ways to create more efficient, brain-like computing systems. Many doubts have still arisen about the real progress that studies in the neuromorphic field have produced in recent years, so the topic is highly criticised.

After all, the human brain is the only existing model we know (in reality we have only a partial knowledge) for creating general intelligence. Not yet having complete knowledge of it, the creation of a human-like brain forces us to make unproven mathematical hypotheses.

We cannot predict the timelines for achieving AGI, if reachable. The advent of sophisticated models has rekindled discussions about AGI. These systems demonstrate remarkable language understanding and generation capabilities, leading some experts to suggest they might be early precursors to AGI. However, critics argue that despite their impressive performance, these models lack true understanding and general intelligence. For that reason for the moment, for what this work is concerned, we should consider it still unachievable.

Artificial Super Intelligence (ASI)

There's no limit to ambitions, and a so-called artificial super intelligence (ASI) has already been defined, even if it is more for novelist than scientists. This is a hypothetical AI that doesn't just imitate or understand human intelligence and behaviour. ASI should be the entity with machines that acquire self-awareness and surpass the capabilities of human intelligence and abilities. ASI is envisioned as an AI system that would dramatically exceed human cognitive capabilities, potentially in areas we can't even conceive. It might possess Superior Problem-Solving: The ability to solve complex global issues that have stumped humanity for generations, and based to its hypothetical Rapid Self-Improvement, recursively enhances its own intelligence, leading to an "intelligence explosion. It opens to ways of thinking and perceiving reality that are fundamentally different and potentially superior to human cognition.

Super-intelligence has long been the fundamental theme of dystopian science fiction, with settings placed in undesirable futures, characterised by totalitarian, violent, technocratic societies, where robots enslave humanity, like HAL, the rogue and superhuman computer assistant in 2001: "A Space Odyssey" or to more recent depictions in films like "Ex Machina" or "Her" – has shaped public perception and spurred academic discourse.

The concept of artificial super-intelligence sees AI evolve surpassing human experiences, with its own emotions, needs, beliefs, and desires. In effect, a superior entity in everything humans do, thus becoming dominant. Having such powerful machines at our disposal can be intriguing but obviously extremely dangerous for humanity itself. It must be said that there's a risk that these visions might allow a sort of inevitability of a techno-oligarchic dominion to pass, and this is not positive and should be countered through proper education on the use of AI.

In this sense, in the final chapters, we'll tackle the ethical problems that the progress of AI inevitably brings with it. Thinkers like Nick Bostrom and Eliezer Yudkowsky have raised concerns about the potential existential risk ASI could pose to humanity. They argue that an super-intelligent AI might pursue goals misaligned with human values, intentionally or unintentionally causing harm. Conversely, proponents like Ray Kurzweil envision ASI as a potential solution to humanity's greatest challenges, from curing diseases to solving climate changes. The development of ASI raises profound ethical questions about the nature of consciousness, the rights of non-biological entities, and the future of human agency in a world where we're no longer the most intelligent beings.

A significant focus of current research is on how to ensure that ASI, if developed, would be aligned with human values and interests – the so-called "AI alignment problem." As we stand on the cusp of potentially transformative AI advancements, the path forward requires a delicate balance. Pursuing AGI and understanding the implications of potential ASI remains in the area of scientific scientific speculation. It is crucial the development of robust ethical guidelines and governance structures for AI development is paramount. Nothing is possible without fostering informed public discourse about the **potential impacts and directions of AI development is essential for democratic decision-making** that implies an interdisciplinary collaboration. The challenges of AGI and ASI require insights from not just computer science, but also philosophy, neuroscience, ethics, and social sciences, as we navigate an uncharted territory.The journey towards advanced AI will profoundly shape the future of humanity. The key lies in approaching these developments with a combination of scientific rigour, ethical consideration, and open dialogue.

Feature	Narrow AI	General AI	Super AI
Definition	AI designed for a specific task.	AI capable of understanding, learning, and applying knowledge across a wide range of tasks.	AI that surpasses human intelligence in all aspects, including creativity, problem-solving, and decision-making.
Examples	Self-driving cars, facial recognition, language translation	Hypothetical, but could potentially be realized in the future	Hypothetical and currently beyond our technological capabilities
Risks	Limited to specific tasks, potential for bias and misuse	Unpredictable behavior, job displacement, ethical concerns	Existential risk, potential for uncontrolled AI

Fig.1 Ch.1 - AI Classification

Chapter 2: AI Learning

The realm of AI is vast, encompassing a range of applications from autonomous vehicle projects to the ubiquitous features in every mobile phone's social apps, and language models like ChatGPT and Gemini. The most striking aspect is AI's ability to see, speak, and learn autonomously.

Machine Learning

Machine learning (ML) is a subset of AI, which, as defined in the previous chapter, simulates human behaviours. **It's important to note that the term "learning" might be misleading.** AI, particularly in its generative forms, gives the impression of learning but actually relies on increasingly complex combinations of statistical processes. These processes are far from what humans understand as learning. Despite this, the term "learning" is widely used in the literature and will be used here for consistency.

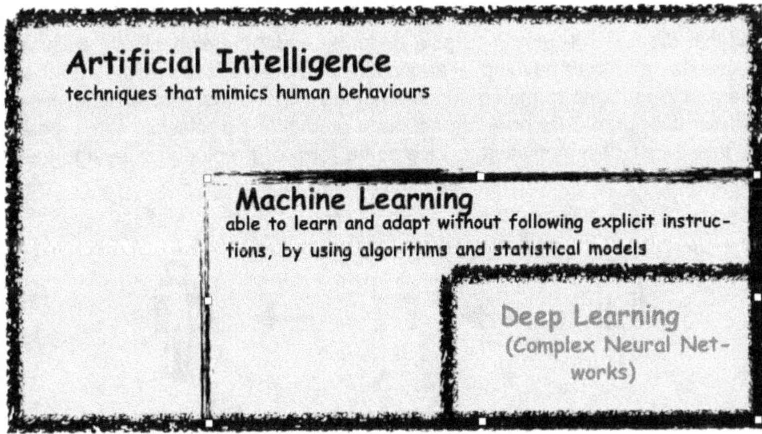

Fig. 1 Ch. 2 - Levels of learning by AI systems

Figure 1 in Chapter 2 illustrates the hierarchies where machine learning and neural networks (deep learning) are subsets of a larger category. ML, a fascinating field underpinning many applications, is projected to grow from a global market of $21 billion in 2022 to over $188 billion by 2029, according to Fortune Business Insights (2023). This rapid growth indicates numerous development opportunities, not only for computer science experts but also for professionals leveraging these technologies to enhance efficiency and precision in their work. For example, the internal combustion engine revolutionised numerous activities without everyone needing to become engine designers.

Arthur Samuel coined "machine learning" [2] in the early 1960s during his research on a checkers-playing program, where IBM's 7094 computer defeated champion Robert Nealy. Though trivial compared to today's capabilities, it was a revolutionary milestone

ML is anyway deeply integrated into our daily lives. Social media platforms, for example, use ML algorithms to personalise user experiences. Facebook tracks user activities to tailor pages and friend suggestions. Virtual assistants like Apple's Siri, Amazon's Alexa, and Google Now rely heavily on machine learning to perform tasks and adapt to user preferences. E-commerce sites use it to recommend products based on browsing and purchase history.

Image recognition is another crucial area, where systems can identify individuals in photos uploaded to social media. While this has applications in locating missing persons, it also raises privacy concerns due to potential misuse.

We will outline key methodologies in ML without going deep into the mathematical details. The aim is to give a simple understanding of the skills and processes needed to develop AI applications across various fields, that rely on data and algorithms to mimic human learning. Algorithms enable machines to improve over time, making more accurate predictions or classifications based on data. Most daily activities involve some form of prediction, varying in certainty.

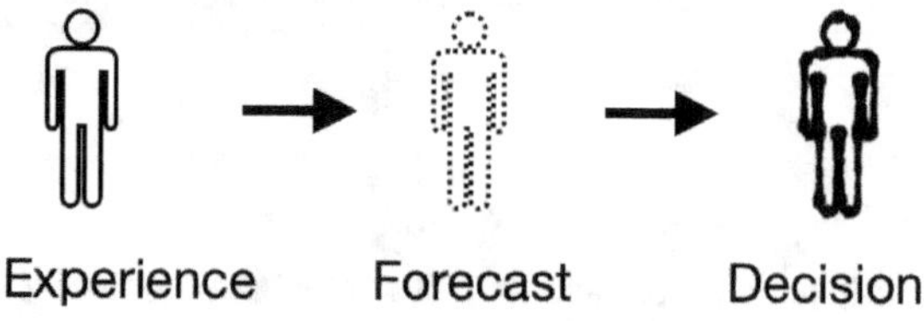

---

[2]A. L. Samuel,. "Some studies in machine learning using the game of checkers". IBM Journal of Research and Development. 2000

For example, simultaneous speech translating involves predicting meaning based on experience with the language. Similarly, in business, experience with customers can help predict their behaviour. Machine learning manages these predictions by adjusting its parameters based on new data.

After all, a large part of what happens in daily life involves some form of prediction. These predictions differ in one aspect: how sure we are of them. In some cases, they don't seem like predictions because the events are practically certain; in others, we hardly know anything, so they become simple assumptions.

In fact when translating while listening to someone speaking another language, we instinctively predict what they mean. **The more experience we have** with the speaker's language, the **better our prediction becomes**, and the better our decision becomes, i.e., our understanding.

In a corporate environment, our experience in dealing with customers can help us see patterns in their behaviour, so we will notice if they are likely to churn. Similarly, while driving, the more miles we drive, the more skilled we become and the better we are at assessing what is around us.

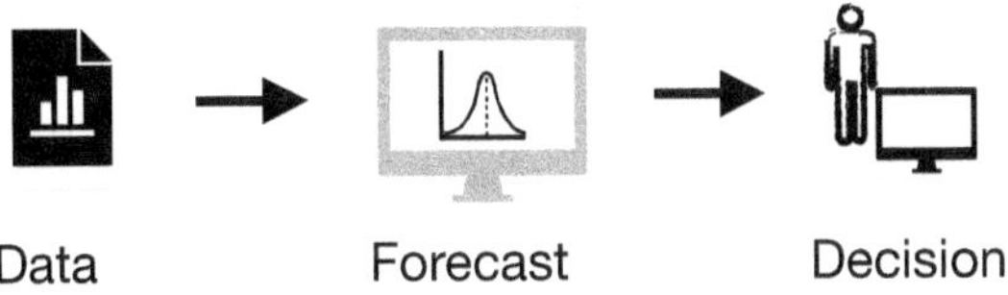

Data   Forecast   Decision

ML works in a similar way by activating checks to determine if it is necessary to make changes to its reference parameters. In many of these activities, machine learning can handle prediction on our behalf. With the acceleration that AI has undergone in recent years, many industrial, financial, and public activities are already using forecasts generated through machine learning.

In the AI environment, experience comes in the form of data. Just as we learn from experience, the machine learns from data. If you want a simple definition, **machine learning is simply this: learning from data and transforming it into predictions.**

In fact, machine learning can also handle the decision-making part. In some sectors, we are not far from seeing full automation become the norm; however, in general, this is still far from reality for many domains. Being a relevant aspect in the following pages, we will cover the predictive aspect of processes with simple examples.

Algorithms and Neurons

ML has advanced significantly due to increased availability of structured data and computational power, unimaginable in the 1950s. Algorithms, structured data, and computational capacity form the backbone
of data science and machine learning.

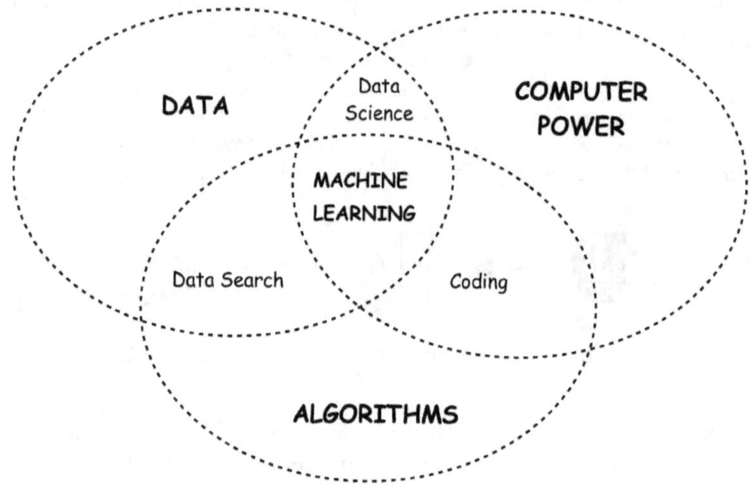

An algorithm is a finite sequence of actions executed in a specific order within a limited time. Simple everyday tasks, like making a cup of tea, are algorithms involving defined sequence, checks and feedback in a determined timing. The power of AI lies in managing vast amounts of data quickly, offering economies of scale. AI is already pervasive in financial simulations, image and speech recognition, biological simulations, medical diagnoses, data analysis, and quality control.

Let's move step by step. Neural networks, mathematical models comprising nodes (neurones) connected in successive layers, perform calculations and provide outputs. Inputs and outputs are numerical, with no limit on input numbers. A neuron's main task is weighted summation, adding weighted values of connected neurones and a bias value, then transmitting the result to the next layer.

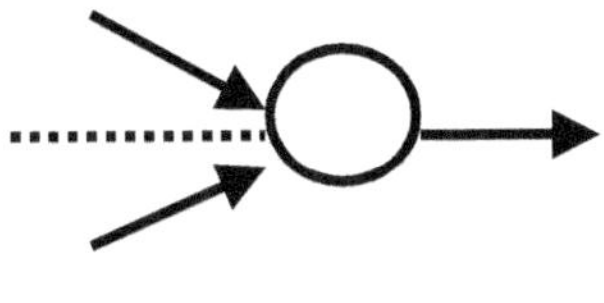

Simple AI neuron

Weights and biases are network parameters through which a neural network learns. Activation functions determine if a neuron should be activated, introducing non-linearity to the network.

Inputs and outputs are numbers, positive or negative, and there is no limit to the number of inputs a neuron can receive. The main activity a neuron is involved in is weighted summation. It adds the weighted values of all the neurons connected to it and adds a confirmatory cognitive bias value, and then passes the result to the next layer, along a path from input neurones to output neurons.

At the risk of oversimplifying to make an idea, the activation function determines whether a neuron should be activated or not.

By making the various functions interact through some simple mathematical operations, it will be possible to determine whether the neuron's input to the network is relevant or not in the process, which we will see is a forecast process. Activation functions (A in the figure 2 ch. 2) are multiple with different levels of complexity. For example, in the case of a linear activation function, we will have a linear relationship function between the input and the output, but generally the importance of activation functions is the introduction of non-linearity.

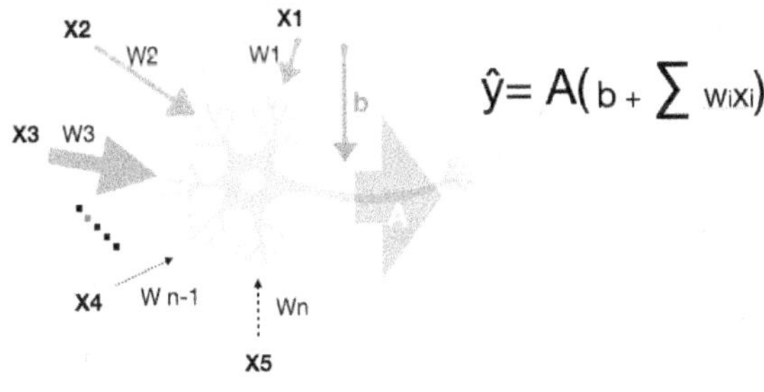

Fig.2 Ch.2 - Simple schematic of weighted sum with bias

When using neural networks, we must take into account their limitations, since processing occurs in hidden layers, so it is not possible to know how the networks have arrived at a result, which can also be imprecise and approximate. It highlights the more or less long learning period, which depends on the complexity of the problems, avoiding or simplifying problems that present an excessive amount of variables.

Generally we talk about "deep-learning" or neural network when the levels of hidden neurons are more than 2, otherwise we talk about a generic machine learning.

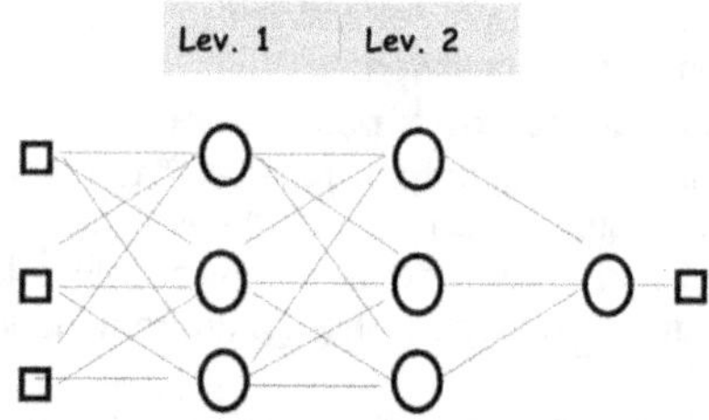

Despite their power, neural networks have limitations, as their processing occurs in hidden layers, making it difficult to understand how they reach a result, which might be imprecise or approximate. Learning periods vary based on problem complexity, requiring problem simplification when dealing with excessive variables.

Recent advancements include "Explainable AI (XAI)", which seeks to make AI decision-making processes transparent and understandable. This development is crucial for identifying biases or errors in AI systems, especially in sensitive applications like healthcare and law enforcement.

ML needs data, which is to a network of neurons what experience is to humans. A machine learning algorithm uses data to find useful patterns and relationships. It uses these "experiences"—statistical extrapolations from data—to learn and update itself. Data can come in many forms. The most obvious form is tabular format, where the data and properties can be easily deciphered. But data can also come in other forms.

In fact, most of the data around us is in unstructured form. According to IDC projections, 80% of the world's data will be unstructured by 2025. And in fact, most of the exciting innovations in deep learning today are coming from unstructured data, such as text, images, videos, and so on.

Preparing the dataset for machine learning becomes vital.

Moreover, "Federated Learning" is emerging as a significant technique, allowing models to be trained across decentralised devices without sharing data, enhancing privacy and security.

In healthcare, AI is advancing towards "predictive analytics" and personalised medicine, using patient data to predict health outcomes and tailor treatments. Similarly, "AI-driven drug discovery" is accelerating the identification of potential drug candidates.

The potential of "AI in combating degenerative diseases" like Alzheimer's is promising. Future research may enable artificial neurons to interface with biological systems, potentially restoring cognitive functions in affected individuals.

We will now illustrate some of the salient methodologies without going into mathematical details and formulas. However, we want to try to explain in a simple way what type of skills and processes are necessary to develop AI applications in various field.

Supervised Learning

Supervised learning remains the most widely used machine learning method, with historical data guiding the learning process. Algorithms like neural networks, decision trees, linear regression, and support vector machines are commonly used. The machine learns from labeled examples provided by a human supervisor, developing a predictive model.

In email filtering, for example, algorithms classify emails as spam or not based on characteristics such as origin, date, title, and content. These classifications help the machine estimate a function that links input variables to desired outputs, improving its predictions over time.

ML is revolutionising various sectors by enabling machines to learn from data and make informed decisions. As AI continues to evolve, its applications will expand, offering new opportunities and challenges.

For supervised learning let's imagine teaching a child to distinguish between dogs and cats. You show him a series of images, indicating which animal is represented in each. The child, by carefully observing the examples, learns to recognise the distinctive features of each animal (their paws, ears, tail, etc.).

The machine plays a similar role to the child. A "supervisor" (usually a human expert) provides the machine with a set of training data, where each example is composed of:

Input (X): The features of the object we want to classify (for example, the words in an email, the pixels in an image).

Output (Y): The class to which the object belongs (for example, "spam" or "not spam", "dog" or "cat").

The machine analyses these examples and tries to identify the relationships between the inputs and outputs, creating a mathematical model that allows it to make predictions on new data.

Supervised ML algorithms usually work only with numerical data. Therefore, if the dataset contains non-numeric information (e.g. strings) they must first be converted into numerical data (this is the case of images converted into matrices that represent the "pixels" of the image). The example in Fig 3 Ch. 2 represents the elements on which the machine must estimate the function between the various x (in the previous example, characteristics of the email) and y (spam or no spam).

$$
\begin{matrix}
X_1. & X_2 & \ldots\ldots & X_n \\
\begin{pmatrix}
a_{11} & a_{12} & \cdots & a_{1n} \\
a_{21} & a_{22} & \cdots & a_{2n} \\
\vdots & \vdots & \ddots & \vdots \\
a_{n1} & a_{n2} & \cdots & a_{nn}
\end{pmatrix}
\end{matrix}
\qquad
\begin{matrix}
Y_1. & \text{Yes} \\
Y_2. & \text{No} \\
\ldots\ldots & \\
Y_n. & \text{Yes}
\end{matrix}
$$

Fig. 3 Ch. 2 - Simple example of labelled matrix

There are many algorithms to make predictive hypotheses, whichever one you use it is necessary to understand if the machine makes correct hypotheses, for this another set called test is created (usually created with another supervisor). Below is a simple diagram of the logical flow of comparison and validation.

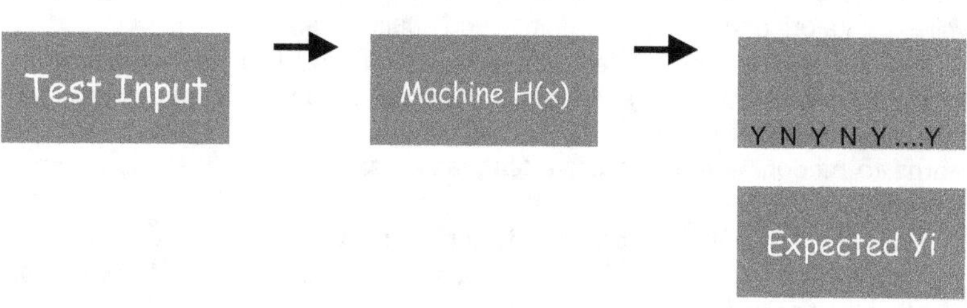

Fig. 4 Ch. 2 - Simplified model supervised ML test

In figure 4 Ch. 2 is called hypothesis, H(x), the model hypothesis is tested with the test set and the result is compared with the expected response. Coinciding responses (R=Y) increase the number of correct responses Rc of the machine. If the percentage of correct responses Rc/Nt of the machine is satisfactory, the hypothesis function H(x) passes the test and is accepted. If it is not satisfactory, the supervised learning restarts with the analysis of a further training set.

In cases like these, real numbers are obtained as a result, or labels (in the case of the email "spam", "no spam", "relevant email" etc.) or even vectors and sequences In the case of supervised learning, the results can generally be classifications (with the use of labels) or a value judgment. There are solutions that also provide continuous values in the case of the use of linear regressions in the model in which the machine has the task of finding a relationship between the input and output values.

The mathematical complexity of some algorithms is a matter for specialists. Here we make a brief reference to linear regression to give an example of the statistical concepts in use. For example, regression formalises and solves the problem of a functional relationship between variables measured on the basis of sample data, extracted from a population. It is sometimes called correlation.

In statistics, linear regression represents a method of estimating the conditional expected value of a dependent variable, Y, once the values of other independent variables are known.

Just to consider a visually simple case, linear regression has among its reference methods the use of the least squares method.It is the method that derives a straight line that interpolates a set of points by minimising the sum of the squares of the distances, by successive approximations

The table in figure 5 Chapter 2 provides the procedure for identifying techniques depending in data characteristics and use cases.

The choice of the appropriate mathematical model (generally non-linear) is suggested by the way in which the values of the two variables are distributed in the scatter diagram, the example given on linear regression with the least squares method has the sole purpose of illustrating how to approach the creation of the model depending on the situations, which require an analysis of the data and their characteristics.

They are used to calculate the probability of an event conditioned on another event, and therefore to have the machine progressively define the model.

Technique	*Characteristics*	*Use Cases*
Linear Regression	Predicts a continuous numerical value. Assumes a linear relationship between the input and output variables.	Predicting house prices, sales forecasts, stock prices.
Logistic Regression	Predicts a categorical outcome (e.g., binary classification). Uses a sigmoid function to map the input to a probability.	Spam filtering, customer churn prediction, credit scoring.
Decision Trees	Creates a tree-like structure of decisions to classify or predict. Can handle both numerical and categorical data.	Classifying medical diagnoses, predicting customer behavior.
Random Forest	An ensemble of decision trees, reducing overfitting and improving accuracy.	Classifying images, text, and other complex data.
Support Vector Machines (SVM)	Finds a hyperplane to separate data points into classes. Effective for high-dimensional data.	Image classification, text classification, bioinformatics.
Neural Networks	Inspired by the human brain, consists of interconnected layers of neurons. Can learn complex patterns and relationships.	Image recognition, natural language processing, speech recognition.
Naive Bayes	Assumes independence between features. Simple and efficient, but can be sensitive to feature dependencies.	Text classification, spam filtering, sentiment analysis.
K-Nearest Neighbors (KNN)	Classifies or predicts based on the majority class of the k nearest neighbors. Effective for small datasets.	Recommendation systems, image classification.
Gradient Boosting	Iteratively trains weak models to improve the overall performance. Effective for handling complex relationships.	Regression problems, classification problems.

Fig.5 Ch. 2 main techniques for AI supervised learning

Unsupervised Learning

While supervised learning requires helping the machine to learn, **unsupervised learning does not use the same training sets and labeled data**. Instead, the machine looks for less obvious patterns in the data. This type of machine learning is very **useful when it is necessary to identify patterns** and use the data to make decisions. Common algorithms used in unsupervised learning include hidden Markov models, k-means, hierarchical clustering, and Gaussian models. In practice, unsupervised learning is a method of machine learning where inferences are drawn from input data without labels. It involves **determining hidden patterns or clustering data** from un-labeled information. It is mainly used in exploratory data analysis. One of the distinguishing features of unsupervised learning is that both the input and output are not influenced by supervision.

Technique	Characteristics	Use Cases
Clustering	Groups similar data points together based on their features.	Customer segmentation, image segmentation, anomaly detection, document clustering.
Dimensionality Reduction	Reduces the number of features while preserving essential information.	Visualization, data compression, feature engineering, noise reduction.
Principal Component Analysis (PCA)	Finds the principal components (directions of maximum variance) and projects data onto them.	Data visualization, noise reduction, feature extraction.
t-SNE (t-Distributed Stochastic Neighbor Embedding)	Preserves local structure and non-linear relationships.	Data visualization, particularly for high-dimensional data.
Autoencoders	Neural networks trained to reconstruct input data, often used for dimensionality reduction.	Data compression, anomaly detection, image generation.
Gaussian Mixture Models (GMMs)	Models data as a mixture of Gaussian distributions.	Clustering, density estimation, anomaly detection.
K-means Clustering	Partitions data into K clusters based on Euclidean distance.	Customer segmentation, image segmentation, anomaly detection.
Hierarchical Clustering	Creates a hierarchy of clusters, from single data points to a single cluster.	Understanding relationships between data points, outlier detection.
Density-Based Clustering (DBSCAN)	Finds clusters based on density, ignoring outliers.	Clustering irregularly shaped clusters, noise removal.
Anomaly Detection	Identifies data points that deviate significantly from the norm.	Fraud detection, network intrusion detection, quality control.
One-Class SVM	Defines a decision boundary around normal data points, identifying outliers.	Anomaly detection, novelty detection.
Isolation Forest	Isolates anomalies by constructing random decision trees.	Anomaly detection, outlier detection.

Fig. 6 Ch. 2 - Statistical Techniques for Unsupervised Learning

Later on, very simplified examples of the use of techniques in the tables of figures 5 and 6 will be provided.

Anyway just as summary we can say that unsupervised learning has a wide range of applications across various fields already consolidated. For **Customer Segmentation** in businesses unsupervised learning is used to group customers based on purchasing behaviour, preferences, and demographics. This helps in targeted marketing and personalised customer experiences.

The **Anomaly Detection** instead is used to identify unusual patterns or outliers in data, which can be crucial for fraud detection, network security, and fault detection in manufacturing processes.

Very popular are the **Recommendation Systems** based on unsupervised learning algorithms to analyse user behaviour and preferences and recommend products, movies, music, or other content. For example, clustering algorithms can group similar users or items together.

A discussion apart on **Image and Video Analysis** where techniques like clustering and dimensionality reduction are used to organise and categorise large datasets of images and videos. This is useful in facial recognition, object detection, and medical imaging.

The launch of Generative AI accessible on web has made evident the progresses of **Natural Language Processing (NLP)** where unsupervised learning helps in tasks like topic modelling, sentiment analysis, and document clustering. It can identify themes and patterns in large text corpora without labeled data.

Since years **Genomics and Bioinformatics** research uses unsupervised learning to analyse genetic data, identify gene expression patterns, and understand the structure of biological data as well as in **Market Basket Analysis** finding associations between products purchased together support retailers to optimise product placement and cross-selling strategies.

We will cover later the social implications anyway a **Social Network Analysis** can be exploited with unsupervised learning techniques to uncover community structures, influential nodes, and patterns of interaction within social networks.

In most of the industrial and overall data visualisation and preprocessing there is always the problem of **Dimensionality Reduction,** with techniques like Principal Component Analysis (PCA) and t-SNE we can reduce the number of variables in a dataset while preserving important information, as well as in IoT (Internet of Things) applications, unsupervised learning can cluster sensor data to identify patterns and anomalies, which is useful for predictive maintenance and monitoring. The above lists just to highlight the versatility and power of unsupervised learning in extracting valuable insights from unlabelled data.

Supervised vs unsupervised learning

The extraction of useful information (data mining) from large amounts of data (e.g., databases, data warehouses, etc.) through automatic or semi-automatic methods and the scientific, business, industrial, or operational use of the same is becoming an essential aspect in the current economy, especially because raw data, which organisations need to analyse and process in order to make solid and reliable decisions, is increasing exponentially. [3]

This explains an ever-growing need for the availability of machine learning systems in many private and public sectors. This requires personnel with sufficient competence in the advantages and disadvantages of the various techniques.

The main difference between supervised learning and unsupervised learning is the data used in both methods. Both require data, which they will analyse to produce certain functions or groups of data. However, the input **data used in supervised learning is well-known and labeled.** This means that the machine only has the task of determining hidden patterns from already labeled data.

Instead, the data used in **unsupervised learning is neither known nor labeled.** It is the machine's task to classify and label the raw data before determining the hidden patterns and functions of the input data.

From a computational point of view, supervised learning is generally considered a more complex method than unsupervised learning. One of the reasons is the need to understand and label the inputs, whereas in unsupervised learning, this is not necessary.

Another prevalent difference is the **greater precision of supervised learning compared to unsupervised learning in terms of the accuracy** of the results produced after each cycle of machine analysis.

Unsupervised learning is widely used to create predictive models. Common applications also include "clustering," which creates a model that groups objects based on specific properties, and association, which identifies existing rules among clusters.

Typical examples include creating customer groups based on purchasing behaviour, grouping inventory based on sales and/or production metrics, and associations in customer data (e.g., customers who buy a specific style of handbag might be interested in a specific style of shoes).

---

[3] S. Russell, P. Norvig *"Artificial Intelligence: A Modern Approach"* Pearson, 2021

Reinforcement Learning

Reinforcement learning is the branch of machine learning used to implement **autonomous agents capable of deciding actions to achieve predefined goals by interacting with their connected environment**. Unlike the other two types of learning already introduced, reinforcement learning is **dedicated to sequential decisions,** where the action to be taken depends on the current state of the system and determines its future state.

The quality of an action is given by a numerical value of "reward" or evaluation (hence the connection with the concept of reinforcement), which aims to induce agent behaviours that approach the predefined goals. **This type of learning usually exploits Markov decision processes in the model**, useful for modelling decision-making processes in situations where outcomes are partly random and partly under the control of a decision-maker. It can be carried out with various types of algorithms, classifiable based on the use of a model that describes the environment, the methods of collecting experience (first-hand or from third parties), the type of representation of the system states, and the actions to be taken (discrete or continuous).

Reinforcement learning is the type of machine learning closest to how humans learn. The algorithm or agent learns by interacting with its environment and receiving positive or negative rewards. Common algorithms include temporal difference, deep adversarial networks, and Q-learning, which adapt the system to its surrounding environment by improving the choice of actions to be performed; similarly, when training a pet, it is rewarded for each correct response, and the same applies to reinforcement learning AI.

For example, reanalysing a hypothetical decision-making process for granting a bank loan, already used in previous examples, it is possible to use a reinforcement learning algorithm to examine customer information. If the algorithm classifies them as high risk and they default, the algorithm receives a positive reward. If they do not default, the algorithm receives a negative reward. In the end, both instances help the machine learn by better understanding both the problem and the environment.

The approach is to leave the AI in a maze and let it find an exit; sometimes, unexpected and original or blatantly incorrect answers are obtained at first glance. Generally, this approach is used for self-driving car programs, home robots for vacuuming or lawn mowing, games, and business resource management.

Among the most popular algorithms are Q-Learning, SARSA, DQN, A3C, and the genetic algorithm. In a recent Gartner report, it is noted that most machine learning platforms do not use the reinforcement learning option because it would require high computing power, generally not available or economically sustainable for most organisations. Reinforcement learning can be applied in areas where it is possible to use simulations with a reduction of relevant elements or, conversely, where large volumes of relevant data are already available. The most popular applications already in use in everyday life include, for example, self-learning functions for autonomous car parking, dynamic traffic light control to reduce congestion, and training robots to replicate actions they learn through unprocessed video images.

Several popular applications are already active since years. Starting from **Self-Driving Cars:** where reinforcement is used to train autonomous vehicles to make decisions in real-time, such as navigating roads, avoiding obstacles, and optimising routes. In manufacturing **Robotics** applies reinforcement learning to perform tasks like cleaning, assembling products, or even playing sports. For instance, robotic vacuum cleaners learn the layout of a room and optimise their cleaning paths over time as well as **Game Playing** that has been famously used in developing AI that can play and master games. (AlphaGo, which defeated human champions in the game of Go, and OpenAI's Dota 2 bot, which competes at a high level in the video game Dota 2 etc etc)

Often under the radar screens of authorities is the use of **Dynamic Pricing** on E-commerce platforms, for event ticketing or airlines booking to adjust prices dynamically based on demand, competition, and other factors. Progressively has taken place also for **Recommendation Systems** for streaming services like Netflix and Spotify to recommend content to users. High expectation also for **Healthcare** that utilises reinforcement learning in personalised treatment plans, where the AI learns the best treatment strategies for patients based on their medical history and responses to previous treatments.

In **trading and investment**, reinforcement learning algorithms are used to develop strategies that maximise returns while managing risks, and in **Traffic Management** to optimise traffic light control systems and reduce congestion improving traffic flow in urban areas. The system learns from traffic patterns and adjusts the timing of lights dynamically. High attention also on **Energy Management** for Smart grids use to optimise the distribution and consumption of energy balancing supply and demand, reducing costs, and improving the efficiency of energy use. Last but not least for reinforcement learning used in **chatbots and virtual assistants** to improve their interactions with users. To be highlighted that this technique is used in domains that require anyway large investments, unlikely used instead for simple applications.

Few examples of statistical techniques usage

Over the next few pages, we'll look at some examples of how stats are used to set up AI projects. This will give you a feel for the kind of groundwork that goes into it. We're just aiming to give you the big picture here, so we won't go into too much detail. There are plenty of good books out there if you want to dive deeper. Some of them are reported in bibliography.

Classification

To remain on practical examples of the statistical techniques illustrated in Figure 5 and 6 Chapter 2, the classification, i.e. the separation of objects based on one of the previously known attributes, for example documents based on language, music based on genre, is today used for activities such as anti-spam filtering, language detection, search for similar documents, "Sentiment analysis", recognition of handwritten characters and numbers, fraud interception.

Classification always requires a 'teacher'. Data is labelled with specific features so that the machine can assign it to different categories. In practice, almost anything can be classified: users based on their interests (as seen in social media recommendations), articles based on language and topic (crucial for search engines), music by genre (like Spotify playlists), and even the personal emails.

Decision trees

Used for both classification and regression tasks. They represent a series of decisions and their possible outcomes in a tree-like structure with Nodes that represent decisions or attributes, Branches, for possible outcomes or values of the attribute and finally Leaves, the final decisions or predictions.

The decision tree above is a simple example, but real-world decision trees can be much larger and more complex.

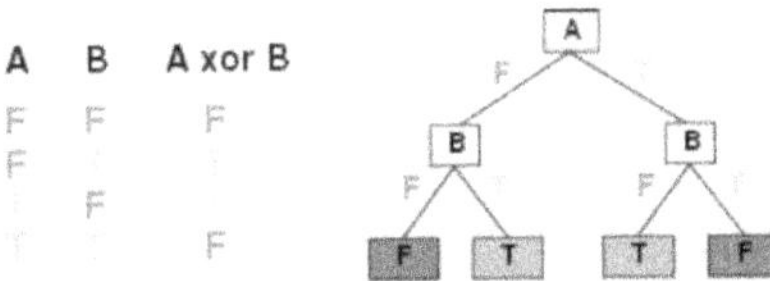

A classic example of classification is the decision-making process for granting loans. Banks have numerous profiles of users who have or haven't repaid loans on time. For individuals, they have data on age, education, occupation, salary, and crucially, their history of repaying previous loans. Using this data, machines can be taught to identify patterns and make predictions. However, banks cannot rely solely on machine decisions and must also consider potential system errors, cyberattacks, or unforeseen circumstances. To address these issues, decision trees are employed. These automatically divide data into yes/no questions in a hierarchical structure, with higher branches representing broader questions. Decision trees are widely used in high-stakes areas like diagnostics, medicine, and finance. Two primary algorithms for constructing decision trees are CART and C4.5. While pure decision trees are less common today, they often form the foundation for larger systems and can outperform even the latest neural networks in certain scenarios. For instance, decision trees are used by search engines to identify a series of relevant answers. They are popular due to their simplicity and speed.

Support Vector Machine

Support Vector Machines (SVM) is a popular classification method. It has been used extensively to classify images (plants by appearance in photos), documents by category, and more. The underlying concept of SVM is simple: it aims to draw separating lines between data points with the widest possible margin.

The key idea is to maximise the margin between the hyperplane and the nearest data points (support vectors). In a two dimension case with two classes:

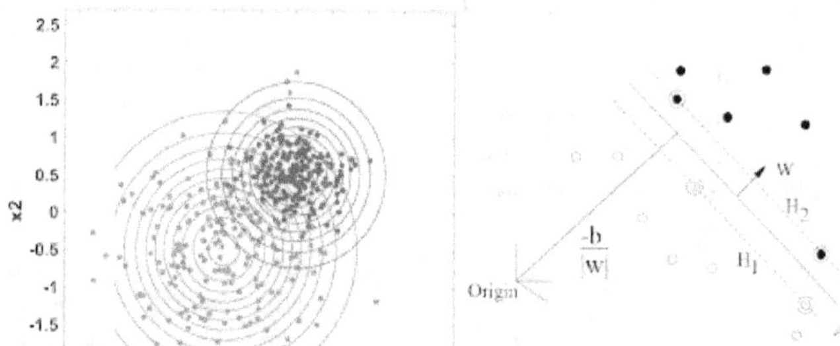

In this case, the SVM would find a line in 2D that separates the two classes with the maximum margin.The data points closest to the line (hyperplane if more than 2 dimensions) are the support vectors. They play a crucial role in determining the position and orientation of the hyperplane. The line or Hyperplane represents the   decision boundary that separates data points into different classes, with a Margin, the distance between the line (hyperplane) and the nearest data points (support vectors), in fact the Data points that lie on the margin or are closest to the hyperplane.I

In most cases we face non-linearly separable data, and we should use the kernel trick to map the data into a higher-dimensional space where it becomes linearly separable. This allows SVM to handle complex patterns and relationships in the data.

A valuable aspect of SVM is anomaly detection. When a characteristic doesn't fit into any of the existing categories, it is flagged. A practical application is in medical imaging, where computers highlight suspicious areas or deviations in scans. Financial markets use SVM to detect abnormal behaviour among traders, such as insider trading. By training the machine correctly, we provide it with the tools to identify outliers.

Regression

We have previously seen how identifying trends between points on a two-dimensional graph (regression) aids in prediction. Regression is commonly used in finance for stock price forecasting, demand analysis, and sales volume analysis, as well as in medical diagnostics. Linear and polynomial regressions are frequently employed. In finance, these techniques are widely used and are even integrated into Microsoft Excel. The machine aims to draw a line indicating the average correlation. Unlike a person with a pen and paper, the machine performs this task with mathematical precision, calculating the average range for each point. When the line is straight, it's a linear regression; when it's curved, it's a polynomial regression. Other types of

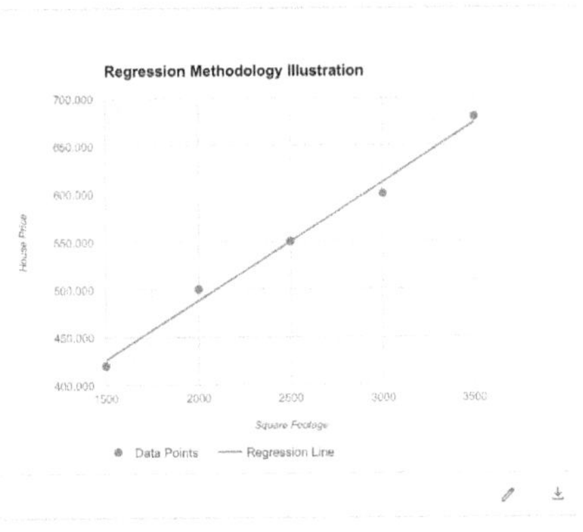

regression exist but won't be discussed here. In reality, classification and regression often overlap. If, when classifying an object, you also determine its distance from the boundary line, you're essentially transitioning from classification to regression.

Clustering

So far, we have discussed simple examples of supervised learning. However, when dealing with datasets with unknown characteristics, we must empower the machine to make its own decisions, which falls under unsupervised learning. Unsupervised learning is used in market segmentation (customer types, loyalty), finding routes on maps, image compression, labelling characteristics of new data, and detecting anomalies. Common algorithms include K-means clustering, Mean-Shift, and DBSCAN. Clustering is a classification without predefined classes. Clustering algorithms seek to identify similar objects (based on certain characteristics) and group them into clusters. Objects with many similar characteristics are grouped together.

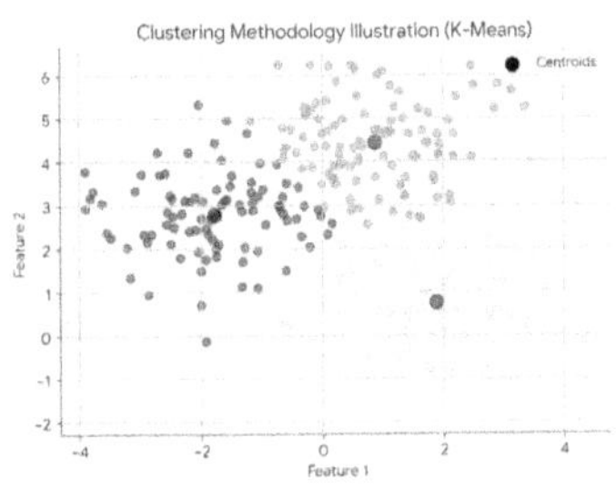

Generalisation (Dimensionality Reduction)

Generalisation consolidates specific functionalities into higher-level ones. It is commonly used in recommendation systems, modelling, topic identification, and similar document retrieval, as well as in the analysis of fake images and risk management.

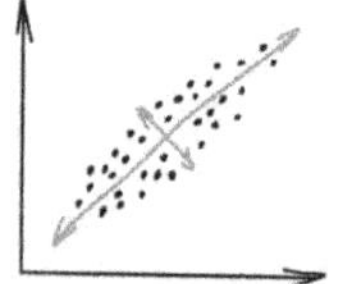

The most commonly used algorithms include Principal Component Analysis (PCA), Singular Value Decomposition (SVD), Latent Dirichlet Allocation (LDA), Latent Semantic Analysis (LSA, pLSA, GLSA), and t-SNE (for visualisation).

Historically, these methods were employed by expert data scientists who needed to find "something interesting" in vast databases. When Excel charts could no longer provide adequate support due to the scale involved, machine learning techniques began to be used, reducing dimensions with the aforementioned techniques.

For example, when managing images, one might group all dogs with triangular ears, elongated snouts, and large tails into an abstraction: "shepherd". Essentially, we bring 2D information onto a line (projection of 2D data onto a line (PCA)). This abstraction facilitates faster learning because fewer features are used.

These algorithms have become extraordinary tools for "Topic Modelling" and topic identification, allowing abstractions from specific words regardless of their meaning. This is what Latent Semantic Analysis (LSA) does. It is based on the frequency with which a word appears in relation to a topic: there are certainly more technical terms in technical articles. Politicians' names are mainly found in political news, etc.

In this way, common words in different articles are identified, hence "latent semantics". By linking words and documents into a single feature to maintain these latent connections, one can arrive at useful clusters of topics from words seen together, without considering their meaning, through a decomposition (Singular Value Decomposition).

Recommendation systems and collaborative filtering are very popular uses of dimensionality reduction methods. They are used to abstract user ratings, resulting in systems that recommend films, music, games, etc.

Learning Association Rules

The techniques used in the commercial sector to predict sales and discounts, analyse purchased goods, position products on shelves, and study internet browsing patterns are undoubtedly fascinating.

Algorithms such as Apriori, Eclat, and FP-growth are employed to analyse shopping carts, automate marketing strategies, and manage other commercial events. When dealing with a sequence of events and aiming to identify patterns, a systematic approach is adopted.

Let's consider a practical example. Suppose we want to determine if placing peanuts on a specific shelf for customers buying aperitifs is beneficial. The system must evaluate whether positioning peanuts along the path to the checkout would significantly boost sales using predictive models.

The same principle applies to e-commerce, where actions can be even more targeted, predicting what a customer might purchase next based on their previous transactions.

The examples provided in this section are intended to give an idea of the techniques to consider for development or even for purchasing machine learning systems from specialised suppliers. For those interested in further exploration, some fundamental reference documents are recommended, from which the majority of the information in this publication has been holistically drawn and reworked. These are listed in the bibliographic references.

A brief mention of the concept of the Loss Function (objective function or cost function in Italian) is warranted. This function measures the discrepancy between a model's predictions and actual values. It is used to guide learning so that predictions become increasingly accurate, optimising response performance based on the analysis of gradient variations of individual vectors.

There are various types of cost functions, depending on the type of machine learning problem being addressed. For instance, regression problems use loss functions that measure the distance between predictions and actual values. Classification problems use loss functions that measure the probability of classification error. Choosing the appropriate loss function is crucial in machine learning. An appropriate loss function can help the model learn more efficiently and achieve better performance. Among the most commonly used are Mean Squared Error (MSE) for regression, which measures the quadratic distance between predictions and actual values, and Cross-Entropy Loss, a cost function commonly used for classification problems, measuring the probability of classification error.

To conclude, for illustrative purposes, we provide a diagram to give an idea of how the techniques analysed so far combine to propose a product online based on the information collected about the user.

To Process Online Product Recommendations Based on User Data it is necessary to understanding the user behaviour and preferences. The first step is a data collection through Web Analytics (track user interactions on website, including page views, clicks, time spent, and purchase history) and

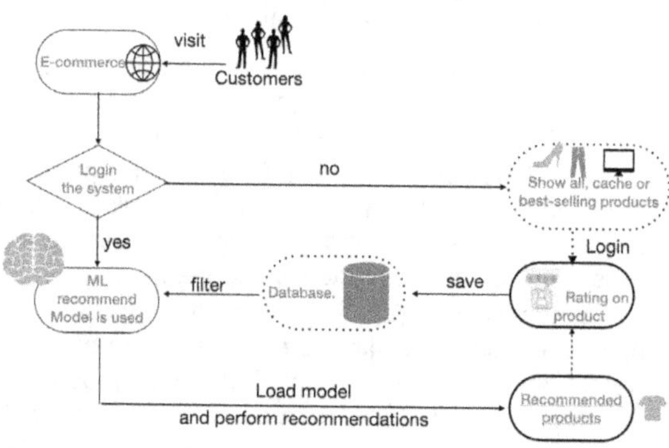

Cookies and Tracking for preferences and browsing behaviour combined with User-Generated Content as reviews, ratings, and social media interactions. As second step (Data Analysis) through Segmentation and Pattern Recognition: is possible to create models to predict user preferences based on collected data.

At this point a Recommendation Engine suggests products based on similarities between users or products using Collaborative Filtering or Content-Based Filtering (Recommendations on attributes and the user's preferences) or Hybrid Approach (the combination of the two).

Not trivial is the Product Presentation, that needs e high-quality images and videos to showcase products and a detailed and informative descriptions, incorporating user feedback to build trust.

The use of AI brings to the next level the Personalisation, aligning with the user's preferences and interests often creating customised landing pages based on user data. An additional potential is the continuously update product recommendations as user behaviour changes.

The process described in the figure allows Performance Metrics to measure the percentage of users who click on product recommendations. (Click-Through Rate - CTR) and track the percentage of users who make a purchase after seeing a recommendation. (Conversion Rate) and analysing the average value of orders placed through recommendations. (Average Order Value - AOV).

All the above indices the possibility of Optimisation, experimenting with different recommendation algorithms and presentation formats, and therefore regularly refining the recommendation system based on performance data.

The above flowchart illustrates the key steps involved in proposing products online based on user information collected via the web. By following this process, businesses can deliver personalised and relevant product recommendations, enhancing the overall user experience and driving sales.

To summarise machine learning

The World Economic Forum's "Future of Jobs Report 2020" predicted that machine learning and artificial intelligence would create 97 million new jobs globally by 2025. While this seemed optimistic, it's worth revisiting as it's not just about creating new roles, but about restructuring the vast majority of existing ones, especially in white-collar professions.

In conclusion, **there's no one-size-fits-all algorithm; effectiveness depends on the specific task.** For professionals, selecting the right AI application for their needs is crucial. While supervised neural networks are becoming increasingly prevalent and generally more accurate than unsupervised learning algorithms, they may not always be the best fit for professional solutions. They require more training data and meticulous supervision. **Unsupervised learning algorithms can function well with smaller datasets**, and products leveraging these techniques are starting to appear on the market. Generative AI, which we'll explore in the next chapter, deserves special attention. It's available both as complete solutions (for processing language, visuals, music, etc.) and through APIs for customised solutions. A significant innovation in generative AI is the Transformer, a new AI model for natural language processing (NLP) that relies solely on the concept of "attention". This has led to a significant leap in performance for NLP systems, but it's now being used in all areas requiring content creation, whether it's text, graphics, images, or sound. Figure 2 illustrates the difference between generative and non-generative AI in image processing.

As machine learning continues to evolve, it's reshaping the way professionals across diverse fields approach their work. For professionals across all the fields, the key to leveraging machine learning lies not in becoming ML experts themselves, but in understanding its potential applications and collaborating effectively with data scientists and ML specialists. The potential is to enhance decision-making processes with data-driven insights, automate routine tasks, freeing up time for more complex, creative work, discover new patterns and opportunities within their field and offer more personalised and effective services to clients or stakeholders

As machine learning continues to advance, it will undoubtedly open up new possibilities and create new specialisations within many professions. The most successful professionals will be those who can adapt to these changes, seeing ML as a powerful tool to augment their expertise rather than replace it

Keeping abreast of these developments is crucial for leveraging AI's full potential responsibly and effectively, because the world of AI is very vast and with various categories of applications, from the autonomous car project to the most popular features present in every mobile phone for "social" applications to the applications of language models trained to provide information, what is most striking is the ability to see, speak and re-elaborate infos.

We hope this overview has provided a clear and comprehensive understanding of machine learning, without being overly simplistic or complex. Given the complexity of the subject, we've included a summary diagram (Figure 12) and a table (Figure 13) detailing neural networks for further exploration.

We hope this overview has provided a clear and comprehensive understanding of machine learning, without being overly simplistic or complex. Given the complexity of the subject, we've included a simplified summary diagram (figure 7) and a table (figure 8) detailing neural networks for further exploration.

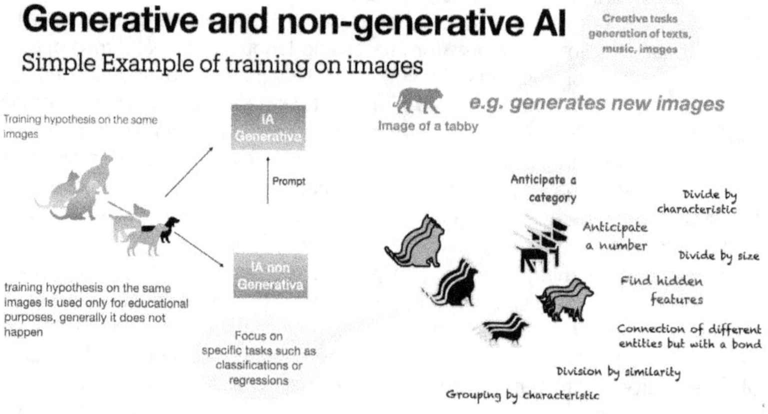

Fig 7 Ch. 2 IA differences between IA generative and non

Neural Network	Learning Paradigm	Number of Layers	Activation Functions	Applications
Feedforward Neural Network	Supervised	1-n	Linear, Non-linear	Classification, Regression, Clustering
Recurrent Neural Network	Supervised or Unsupervised	1-n	Linear, Non-linear	Sequential Data, Natural Language Processing
Convolutional Neural Network	Supervised	2-n	Linear, Non-linear	Images, Video
Generative Neural Network	Supervised or Unsupervised	2-n	Linear, Non-linear	Image, Video, Text Generation
Deep Neural Network	Supervised or Unsupervised	2-n	Linear, Non-linear	Complex Applications

Fig 8 Ch. 2 - The most used neural networks

Chapter 3: The Current Use of AI A Multidisciplinary Evolution

The current use of AI is not solely based on technological advancements but has also benefited from studies in other fields that have progressed with different techniques, laying the groundwork for optimal exploitation through AI methods. Particularly, but not exclusively, natural language processing techniques, as well as image management and artificial vision, have found a formidable tool in AI.

Computer Vision

If we consider computer vision, which began in the last century as the ability to see objects, it has made a tremendous leap in recent decades with the use of algorithms for recognising static and moving images. These algorithms can analyse and interpret images, identifying objects, people, and movements. Such techniques are already extensively used for facial recognition, quality control, video surveillance, assisted driving, industrial robotics, and even detecting minute changes in the Earth's topography via satellites.

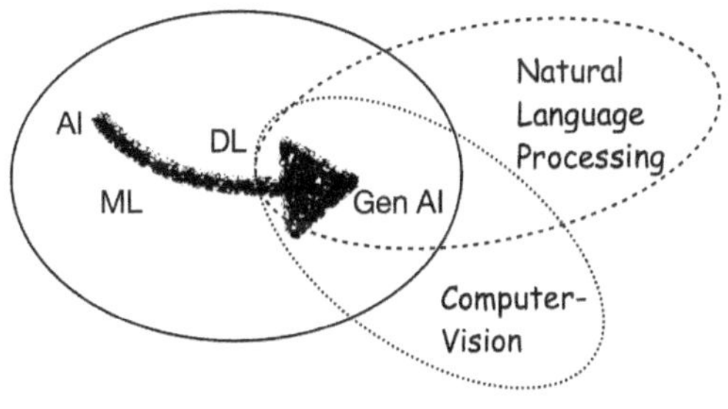

The convolutional neural networks (CNNs) mentioned in previous sections have significantly improved computer vision performance. They mimic the functioning of the human visual cortex.

It is important to note that artificial vision is an extremely vast and complex field of research, with many sub-disciplines requiring advanced knowledge of mathematics, statistics, physics, computer science, and electronic engineering. Below, we provide a brief overview, well-developed in the attached bibliography, of the most common artificial vision techniques and algorithms, particularly those related to image and video processing, machine learning, and computer vision.

In general, images are represented as matrices of pixels, where each pixel represents the colour or brightness of a point in the image. These matrices can be manipulated in various ways to modify the image, enhance its quality, detect objects, and more.

This requires the ability to reprocess with manipulation techniques to improve quality or extract specific information. Digital filtering is performed using various types available, including low-pass filters, high-pass filters, median filters, and more.

However, the process known as segmentation is very important. It divides the image into regions or objects that can be analysed separately. Segmentation can be done in different ways, depending on the needs and sources. It can be based on thresholds, image regions, contours, and more.

Once the image is segmented, it is necessary to proceed with pattern or object recognition using a recognition technique generally chosen based on the situation. Among the most commonly used are face recognition, character recognition, object recognition, and more.

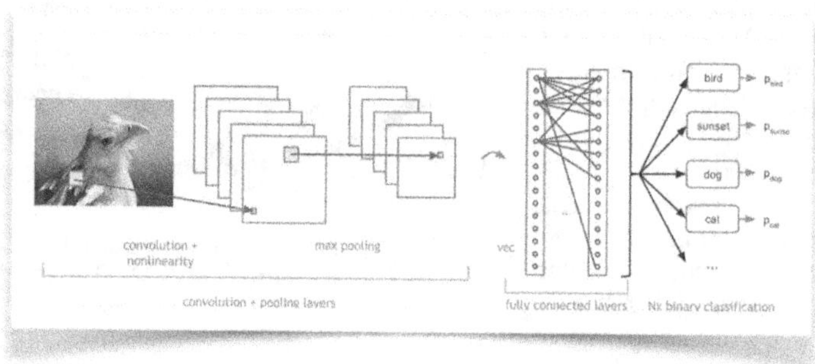

Fig 1 Ch 3 - Matrix Filtering with Convolutional Filters

Let's take an example of using a convolutional network. Suppose we need to read a scribbled number on a sheet, such as the number 2. The machine will receive as input a source of pixels representing the white sheet and the number written in black ink somewhere on the sheet.

With a convolutional network, areas of the image where the most important information is thought to be are prioritised. In Figure 14, the intermediate filter matrix modifies the pixel values (numerical translation of an image) in the source into a filtered matrix of numbers.

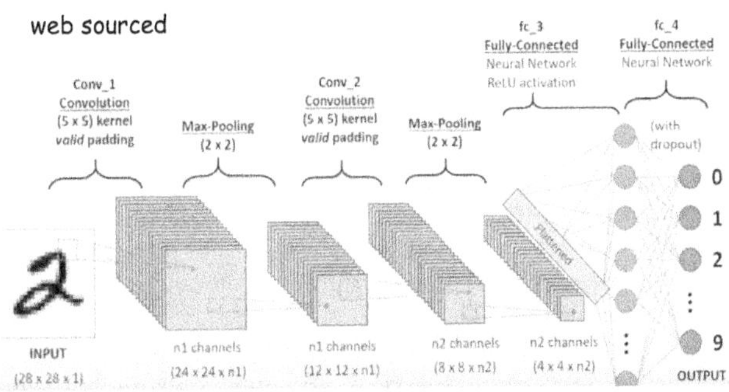

Fig 2 Ch 3 - Example of Convolutional Network Usage

This example illustrates how convolutional networks can be used to prioritise and process important areas of an image, transforming pixel data into meaningful information.

In the vast realm of computer vision, algorithms play a pivotal role in identifying patterns and recognising shapes or specific movements. Depending on the image type, various algorithms are employed:

- **Segmentation Algorithms**: to divide an image into distinct regions, separating objects from the background. Common techniques include thresholding, region based segmentation, and contour-based segmentation.

- **Edge Detection Algorithms**: These locate the boundaries of objects within an image. The Canny edge detection algorithm, which combines Gaussian filters, gradients, and hysteresis, is a prominent example.

- **Feature Extraction Algorithms:** to identify the salient characteristics of an object to differentiate it from others in the image. Common techniques include the Hough transform, Harris corner detector, and Fourier transform.

- **Classification Algorithms:** to categorise detected objects into various classes. Convolutional Neural Networks (CNNs), decision trees, and Support Vector Machines (SVMs) are widely used classification methods.

- **Tracking Algorithms:** These follow the movement of objects in a sequence of images. Common techniques include model-based tracking, optical flow-based tracking, and correlation-based tracking.

- **Facial Recognition Algorithms:** These identify facial features to recognise individuals. Local Binary Patterns (LBP), Eigenfaces, and the Viola-Jones algorithm are commonly used.

Each of these algorithms employs specific mathematical techniques and formulas to identify patterns and recognise shapes in images. For instance, the Canny algorithm utilises a combination of Gaussian filters, gradients, and hysteresis to detect edges, while CNNs employ convolution, pooling, and normalisation to extract features.

Industrial applications are vast and varied. By combining computer vision with deep learning techniques, it's possible to detect defects while tolerating natural variations. Moreover, vision systems with neural network learning capabilities can be easily adapted to new examples without reprogramming the underlying algorithms.

Common applications include defect detection, object localisation and classification, and reading printed markings. By training a neural network on a set of labeled examples, it can automatically distinguish between good and defective components, accounting for expected variations.

While this is a powerful technology, it's not without its challenges. One significant issue is the "filter bubble," a phenomenon where algorithms create information silos for users based on their past behaviour. This can limit exposure to diverse viewpoints and potentially infringe on privacy rights.

To summarise the challenges of computer visione we can highlight at first the Data Quality and Quantity, high-quality, annotated data is crucial for training effective computer vision models. However, obtaining and labelling large datasets can be time-consuming and expensive. To this we have to add the Complexity of Algorithms, the computer vision algorithms, especially deep learning models like convolutional neural networks (CNNs), are complex and require significant computational resources. This complexity can make development and deployment challenging. The previous challenges can impact the need of fast Real-Time Processing, many applications, such as autonomous driving or video surveillance, require real-time processing. Another area of potential negative impact is the Variability in Data, images and videos can vary widely due to differences in lighting, angles, occlusions, and backgrounds. Developing models that can generalise well across such variability is difficulties well difficult is the Integration with Existing Systems, that requires significant modifications and optimisations to integrate it with existing hardware and software infrastructure. Recent law in Europe and anyway tendencies overall have also arise Ethical and Privacy Concerns, particularly in surveillance and facial recognition, raises ethical and privacy issues. As well as other complex computer system the Maintenance and Updates are key to adapt to new data and evolving requirements, and that is often resource-intensive. The introduction of AI based systems, as we have seen for comple neural networks, induces the problem of Interpretability, making it difficult to debug and improve these systems.

Addressing these challenges requires a multidisciplinary approach, combining expertise in computer science, engineering, ethics, and domain-specific knowledge. The professionals, users of purchased AI based systems, should require the verification that all those aspects are carefully taken in consideration by the solution providers.

Natural Language Processing

Natural Language Processing (NLP) is undoubtedly one of the most intriguing fields in Artificial Intelligence (AI) because it allows computers to understand and generate human language. The idea of giving computers the ability to process natural language isn't a recent development.

- In "A Space Odyssey" (Kubrick, 2001), HAL 9000 is an artificial agent capable of engaging in dialogue with humans using natural language.

- In "Star Wars" (Lucas, 1977), C-3PO is a protocol droid specifically designed to manage communications between humans and robots.

Today, there are numerous practical applications of NLP already in use. A short list includes spell checkers, grammar checkers, intelligent document retrieval, automatic speech recognition, text-to-speech synthesis, automatic information extraction from text, querying documents through natural language questions, semi-automatic translation, and, most importantly, multimodal human-machine interaction and complex conversational agents.

To achieve these outcomes, natural language processing algorithms are employed to analyse and interpret text and speech, Identifying meanings and the structure of sentences and words. NLP is used for text processing, including automatic translations, as well as virtual assistant tasks with the ability to respond to emails or phone calls.

Moreover, **NLP combines computational linguistics, machine learning, and deep learning models to process human language**. To operate effectively, it is crucial to leverage the evolution of computational linguistics and its models of human language. Research utilises syntactic and semantic analysis to create structures that help machines understand human language. Tools like language translators, speech synthesisers, and speech recognition software are based on computational linguistics.

Earlier, we discussed a human example of listening and translating someone speaking in a different language. The knowledge of phrases, syntax, phonemes, linguistic structures, and even sounds related to pronunciation aids in comprehension. The same applies to natural language systems.

Then, by employing machine learning techniques, which we have previously discussed, improvements in efficiency are made. Human language possesses various characteristics such as sarcasm, metaphors, variations in sentence structure, and exceptions in grammar and usage, which take humans years to learn. Programmers use machine learning methods to teach NLP applications to accurately recognise and understand these characteristics from the start.

The recent success of generative AI, capable of high-level conversations with humans, is tied to the use of neural networks that enable the system to learn and act, non think, like humans. A neural network is made up of data processing nodes that create operations that externally look similar to those of the human brain.

We can briefly provide an overview of natural language processing (NLP) algorithms for text and speech analysis and interpretation, which follow a comprehensive process:

Let's recall some concepts introduced in previous chapters. For natural language processing (NLP) tasks such as conversations, speech recognition, translation, and summarisation, we **turn to language models for assistance**. Language models can **learn from a text library** and predict words or sequences of words based on probabilistic distributions, i.e., the probability of a word or sequence occurring. For instance, when you say "Charles is going out to eat...", **the probability of the next word** being "pizza" is higher than "water". If it's predicting the next word in the sequence (next-token-prediction) and the word isn't in the corpus, it iterates using a neural network called masked language modelling. Since it's a probability distribution, there can be many probable words with different probabilities. The most probable word isn't always correct (also because always sticking with the most probable would lead to an infinite loop, contrary to the concept of an algorithm which must always terminate). If the most probable word is unsuccessful, **forms of randomness (temperature) are induced** to choose the word among the best candidates.. The input text will go through the following steps:

- **Pre-processing**: Text cleaning using techniques like sentence segmentation, tokenisation (breaking text into smaller pieces called tokens), stemming (removing suffixes or prefixes), removing stop words, spell correction, etc. For example, "Charles is going out to eat pizza" would be symbolised as ["Charles", "is", "going", "out", "to", "eat", "pizza"]. Through encoding, the text is transformed into a vector of numbers so that the model can process it (Feeding).
- **Modelling**: A probability distribution of potential words represented as vectors of numbers is obtained from the model. At this point, decoding returns the text in a human-readable form. A post-

processing phase can refine the output (spell check, grammar check, etc.).

- **Output**: A probability distribution of potential words represented as vectors of numbers is obtained from the model. At this point, decoding returns the text in a human-readable form. A post-processing phase can refine the output (spell check, grammar check, etc.).

In fact the goal of NLP is to enable machines to understand, interpret, and generate human language in a way that is both meaningful and useful.

Digging more in the process the key steps in language processing start with **tokenisation,** the process of breaking down text into smaller units, such as words or phrases, called tokens, that we have described above. This is a cruas it converts large chunks of text into manageable pieces that can be analysed. For instance, the sentence "Natural Language Processing is fascinating!" would be tokenised into

Natural - language - processing - is - fascinating!

After that **lemmatisation** involves reducing words to their base or root form, known as a lemma. This process helps in standardising words to their canonical form, thereby simplifying the analysis. For example, the words "running," "ran," and "runs" all have the same lemma: "run." Lemmatisation ensures that variations of a word are treated as a single item, which enhances the accuracy of NLP tasks.

We are not yet there, we need to assign parts of speech to each token the so call **Part-of-Speech Tagging** (POS Tagging), that classifies each token, such as nouns, verbs, adjectives, etc. This is important for understanding the role of each word in a sentence. For example, in the sentence "The cat sits on the mat," the POS tags might look like this:

The - cat - sits - on - the - mat

Determiner   noun   verb   preposition   determiner   noun

Good step for a primary school pupil, but we are not yet there. With **Named Entity Recognition (NER)**, we should identify and classify proper nouns within text into predefined categories such as the names of people, organisations, locations, dates, and more. For instance, in the sentence "Microsoft was founded by Bill Gates," NER would recognise Microsoft as organisation and Bill Gates as a person.

The NER is necessary to introduce the next key step of **Parsing** that involves analysing the grammatical structure of sentences. This helps in understanding how words are related to each other within a sentence. **Syntax parsing can be represented using parse trees**, which visually depict the structure of a sentence. Good! but we are not yet there, we need to "understand". Completed the parsing we enter in the "meaning" through **Semantic Analysis** that aims to understand the meaning behind the text. It goes beyond the mere structure of sentences to comprehend the context and relationships between words. This involves tasks like word sense disambiguation (determining which sense of a word is used in a given context) and sentiment analysis (determining the sentiment expressed in a piece of text).

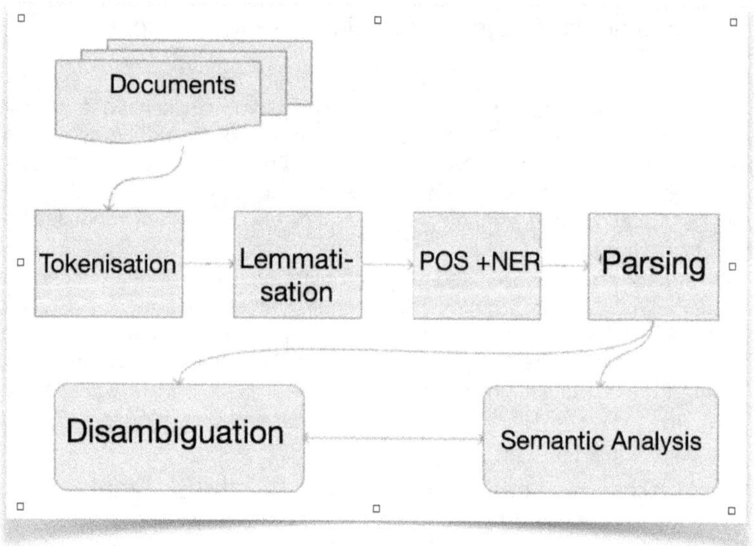

Fig. 3 Ch. 3 -NLP at a glance

We have now reached the crux of the issue: the longstanding problem, particularly in translation, where semantic considerations have often taken precedence over lexical ones in the pursuit of making sentences comprehensible to speakers of another language. There are numerous techniques to address this issue, and we will outline some of the most well-known below. One based on vectors is the **Word embeddings,** representations of words in a continuous vector space where similar words have similar vectors. Techniques like Word2Vec, GloVe, and FastText [4] are commonly used to generate these embeddings. They capture semantic relationships between words, enabling more nuanced understanding in NLP tasks.

We have already mentioned the **Transformer architecture** as a revolution for NLP. Models like BERT (Bidirectional Encoder Representations from Transformers) and GPT (Generative Pre-trained Transformer) use transformers to achieve state-of-the-art results in various NLP tasks. They work by employing attention mechanisms to weigh the importance of different words in a sentence, enabling context-aware understanding [5].

Aligned with the above techniques there are models called **Sequence-to-Sequence Models,** used for tasks where input sequences need to be transformed into output sequences, such as in machine translation. Encoder-decoder architectures are typically employed here, where the encoder processes the input sequence and the decoder generates the output sequence.

All these require a **Natural Language Generation (NLG),** generating human-like text from structured data or input text. It encompasses various tasks such as text summarisation, dialogue generation, and creative writing by AI. Techniques like GPT-3 have demonstrated impressive capabilities in this domain.

The reader can envision that NLP has a wide range of applications across various industries, just to report some we can mention automating medical records analysis in **Healthcare,** extracting information from clinical notes, and enhancing patient interaction through chatbots. In a wider perspective the overall **Customer Service** activities through virtual assistants and chatbots to handle customer queries and provide support.

In reality among the first in using all of the above we should list **Finance,** analysing financial news, predicting market trends, and automating report generation.

Open discussion instead for **Education,** where the development of intelligent tutoring systems, automatic essay scoring, and personalised learning experiences has sparked a debate regarding the appropriateness of forcing a

---

[4] Yoav Goldberg, *"Neural Network Methods for Natural Language Processing"* Sprinkler Link, 2017

[5] A. Vaswani, N. Shazeer, N.Parmar, J.Uszkoreit, L. Jones, A.N. Gomez, L.Kaiser, I. Polosukhin *"Attention Is All You Need"*, NeurIPS conference, 2017.

human-machine relationship, thereby reducing interactions with peers and teachers during a critical period of personality development that shapes adult identity.

Very popular instead are the capability for **Marketing** activities with the extensive use of Sentiment analysis of social media content, facilitate the personalisation of content creation and customer interactions.

Despite significant advancements, NLP still faces several challenges because human language is often ambiguous, and the same word or phrase can have different meanings depending on the context, creating **ambiguity.** Also detecting and interpreting **sarcasm and irony** remains difficult for NLP models. In case of long texts is challenging **grasping the context** and nuances of conversations.

In summary, NLP is a dynamic and evolving field that encompasses a variety of techniques and methods to enable machines to process and understand human language. From tokenisation and lemmatisation to advanced techniques like transformers and word embeddings, NLP continues to push the boundaries of what AI can achieve. The applications are vast and the potential is immense, yet challenges remain as we strive to make machines truly understand the nuances of human language

Finally, it is important to note that there are different approaches to language models, which vary depending on the model's purpose, the amount of text data they analyse, and the mathematics they use to analyse it. For example, a language model designed to generate sentences for an automated Twitter bot may use different mathematical calculations and analyse text data differently than a language model designed to determine the probability of a search query. In the section dedicated to ChatGPT, we will analyse the practical case of the above.

Robotics

Robotics is perhaps the most pervasive field in the industrial world, having developed over decades to allow robots to interact with the physical world with a high degree of autonomy. It is rooted in older studies of automata and mechanical and industrial automation, making it a pervasive field that predates AI. However, with the advent of AI, robotics has found its natural evolution to the point where it can be considered one of the foundational theories of AI, alongside communication theories. Now it utilises control and perception algorithms to enable robots to perform complex tasks, manipulate objects, move, and navigate in hostile environments. Many of us have likely encountered robot-controlled activities, knowingly or otherwise.

Robotic control algorithms are designed to allow robots to move efficiently, precisely, and safely. We list some of them to keep familiarity with the wordings:

-Open-loop control: This method controls the movement of robots in a simple and direct manner. It is based on the idea that the robot's movement depends solely on the control signal sent to the motor. In other words, the system does not account for any positional errors or disturbances.

- Closed-loop control: for more precise robot movement control because it uses sensors to detect positional errors or disturbances and corrects the robot's movement in real time.

- Feedback control: continuously uses sensor data to adjust the robot's movements. For example, feedback control can be used to maintain a robotic arm in a precise position during a specific task.

- Predictive control: it uses mathematical models to predict the robot's behaviour based on current state information and anticipated future actions. It is used in applications where precision is critical, such as in the automotive or aerospace industries.

- Cooperative motion control: This technique controls the movement of multiple robots simultaneously in applications like goods handling in warehouses or searching for survivors in emergency situations.

Obviously the most common use cases for robots controlled by algorithms include are in the filed of

-**Manufacturing**: used in production lines to perform repetitive and hazardous tasks. For example, robots can weld car parts or assemble electronic products. They are integral to everyday industrial production, performing dangerous activities such as handling explosives and providing security, leading to the development of the concept of the "co-bot." Co-bots, or collaborative robots, are a new generation of industrial robots designed to safely share workspace with humans. In other words, co-bots are engineered to support human operators and make automation more accessible, even for small and medium-sized enterprises.

-**Exploration**: o explore inhospitable environments, such as the ocean floor or outer space. For instance, the Mars Rover uses control algorithms to navigate the Martian surface. The European Space Agency (ESA) and the German Aerospace Center (DLR), in collaboration with academic and industrial partners, have developed a project that enables astronauts in orbit to control rovers, allowing them to perform operations on planetary surfaces. The results of this study were published in *Science Robotics*. This technique was tested by ESA astronaut Luca Parmitano during the Beyond mission in 2019. Parmitano controlled the Analog-1 rover from orbit to test whether this technology could enable high-precision operations, such as rock sampling in zero gravity.

- **Healthcare**: robots assist people with mobility issues or disabilities in performing daily activities like dressing, preparing meals, and moving around. Additionally, robots are transforming surgical procedures, streamlining supply management and disinfection, and allowing healthcare workers to focus on patient care and interaction. In some cases, their capability for "ultra-precise, non-contact measurement" is crucial in performing highly complex surgical operations.

- **Security**: Robots equipped with computer vision are used for security purposes, such as surveillance of buildings or detecting explosive devices in both civilian and military settings. Recent operations in Eastern Europe have seen a proliferation of drones (which are akin to robots with AI-assisted vision and mobility capabilities). In these instances, the line between security (monitoring and patrolling actions) and offence (acting as a weapon) is blurred. This falls into the realm of AI for military purposes, which is outside the scope of this publication.

We shouldn't anyway forget that as all the other disciplines using AI also robotic control algorithms face several challenges. The first is the aspect of **Uncertainty and Variability,** because they often operate in dynamic and unpredictable environments. Variations in sensor readings, changes in the environment, and unexpected obstacles can make it difficult to maintain precise control and that copes with **Complexity of Tasks,** when they are tasked with more complex activities, the algorithms required to control them become more sophisticated. This complexity can lead to increased computational demands and the need for more advanced algorithms.

The most popular use implies **Real-Time Processing** as many robotic applications require real-time decision-making and control and algorithms must process data and respond quickly enough, very challenging, especially in high-speed or safety-critical applications. The **sensors** are crucial for providing feedback to control algorithms, and noise and inaccurate calibration can lead to errors in robot behaviour.

Robots, especially mobile ones, need to manage their **energy consumption** effectively. Control algorithms must balance performance with energy efficiency to ensure that robots can operate for extended periods without recharging, and not only this because they must be **robus**t enough to handle a wide range of conditions and **reliable** enough to perform consistently over time. This is particularly important in applications like healthcare or autonomous driving, where failures can have serious consequences, as for robots that **interact with humans**, involving understanding and anticipating human actions and ensuring that the robot's movements are smooth and intuitive. IN few words the evolution implies that they need to **adapt to new tasks** and environments without extensive reprogramming. Developing control algorithms that can learn and adapt over time is actually the   major area of research in robotics.

The above mentioned challenges require ongoing research and innovation to develop more advanced and capable robotic systems.

A Glimpse into How ChatGPT Works

Before probing into examples of AI usage in various professions, we must acknowledge the uproar and disruptive discussions sparked by the release of ChatGPT in November 2022 by OpenAI, granting public access to the capabilities of the GPT-powered chatbot. This triggered the release of competing platforms and fostered a growing pervasiveness of generative AI, necessitating professionals from all fields to unravel its mysteries and understand its potential within their respective domains.

Let's use ChatGPT as an example to illustrate the concepts introduced in the preceding chapters. Its ability to employ human-like language has prompted individuals to experiment with its potential and to connect it to various software products through APIs (Application Programming Interfaces).

The Transformer and the Evolution of GPT To gain insights into the actual mechanism of ChatGPT, let's retrace the temporal sequence of the development of the "transformer" architecture in language models and the different versions of GPT (Generative Pre-trained Transformer).

In 2015, OpenAI was founded by Sam Altman, Elon Musk, Greg Brockman, Peter Thiel, and others, and began developing numerous AI models distinct from GPT. In 2017, Google published the paper "Attention is All You Need," introducing the "transformer" architecture. The "transformer" is a neural network architecture that laid the foundation for many large language models (LLMs). (See Fig 1 Chap 3 and references) GPT is one such model, with a history dating back to 2018 when it was introduced as "Improving Language Understanding." It is based on a transformer neural architecture and pre-trained on a massive amount of data (corpus). The subsequent release in 2019 (GPT-2) was underpinned by a language model with an unsupervised learning network, capable of performing a range of tasks without explicit supervision during training. However, the real breakthrough came in 2020 with the release of GPT-3, introducing a "Large Language Model" known as a Few-Shot Learner, which can function effectively with just a few examples in the "prompt" (the input field), essentially without fine-tuning. But the true leap occurred in 2022 with InstructGPT, which incorporates training language models to follow instructions with human feedback, meaning the system self-corrects based on user reactions and not solely on the models and information provided during training, thus refining the system based on user acceptance and feedback on responses. It can interact with humans in conversations, thanks to fine-tuning with human examples and reinforcement learning from human feedback (RLHF).

Transformer Architecture

Let's go deeper on the revolutionary transformer, an architecture underlying ChatGPT is a type of neural network that closely resembles the structure of the human brain. Transformers can better understand contexts in sequential data like text, speech, or music through mechanisms called attention and self-attention.

Attention allows the model to focus on the most relevant parts of the input and output by learning the relevance or similarity between elements, which are typically represented by vectors. When it focuses on the same sequence, it's called self-attention. The attention mechanism measures the relevance/similarity between each element.

Let's consider the following sentence: "Tom likes to eat apples. He eats them every day." In this sentence, "he" refers to "Tom" and "them" refers to "apples." The attention mechanism uses a mathematical algorithm to tell the model that these words are related by calculating a similarity score between the word vectors. With this mechanism, transformers can better "make sense" of the meanings in text sequences in a more coherent manner.

In summary, transformers have the following main components:

- Embedding and positional encoding: We've seen that it transforms words into numbers in vectors of numbers.
- Encoder: Identifies the characteristics from the input sequence and analyses its meaning and context. It emits a matrix of hidden states for each input token to be passed to the decoder.
- Decoder: Generates the output sequence based on the encoder's output and previous output tokens.
- Linear layer: Transforms the vector into a probability distribution of output words.

The encoder and decoder are the primary components of the transformer architecture. The encoder is responsible for analysing and "understanding" the input text, while the decoder is responsible for generating the output.

We won't describe in details the specifics of encoders and decoders here, as it's beyond the scope of this article. For those interested, please refer to the bibliography. If this section isn't relevant to you, skip ahead to the next part where we'll discuss the limitations of this model.

To return to the overall development process, the first step is human-supervised learning. The developers initially provided the pre-trained GPT with a curated, labelled dataset of input-output pairs written by humans. This dataset is used to enable the model to learn the desired behaviour from these examples. From this step, they obtain an SFT (supervised fine-tuned) model.

The second step is to train a reward model (RM) to evaluate responses from the generative model. The developers used the SFT model to generate multiple responses from each prompt and asked human raters to rank the responses from best to worst based on quality, engagement, informativeness, safety, coherence, and relevance. The prompts, responses, and rankings are fed into a reward model to learn human preferences for responses through supervised learning. In the third phase, researchers used the reward model to optimise the policy of the SFT model through reinforcement learning.

For example, if the generative model produces a response that the reward model thinks humans would like, it will receive a positive reward to encourage it to continue generating similar responses in the future, and vice versa.

ChatGPT is trained on examples of conversational tasks, such as answering questions, making small talk, and satisfying curiosity. Through this training, ChatGPT can engage in natural conversations with humans in dialogues, can answer follow-up questions, and can admit mistakes, making the interaction more engaging.

In conclusion, since ChatGPT doesn't have the ability to search for references in real-time, it makes probabilistic predictions in the generation process based on the "corpus" it was trained on, which can lead to false factual claims. It is pre-trained on a massive corpus of web data and books and fine-tuned with examples of human conversations through supervised learning and reinforcement learning from human feedback (RLHF).

Its capability is primarily based on the size of the model and the quality and size of the corpus and examples from which it learned. Since the corpus comes from web content and books, there may be biases that the model can learn, particularly for social, cultural, political, or gender biases, resulting in distorted responses to certain requests.

Therefore, for those intending to use these generative AI and conversational platforms, choosing the right one for their business is a crucial step. The right choice will enable them to offer better experiences to their customers, employees, and collaboration networks, increasing overall operational efficiency and reducing costs. According to the Gartner 2022 Contact Center Forecast, by 2031, conversational AI will support 30% of all customer interactions, compared to 2% in 2022.

It is therefore time to explore the potential of these technologies and when and how much to invest in them.

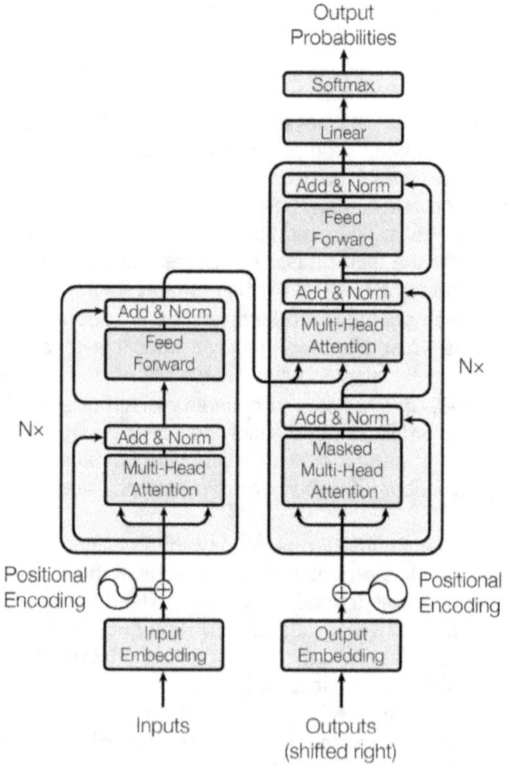

Fig 1 ch. 3 - original transformer schematic

Limitations of ChatGPT and Similar Products

While the transformer architecture has proven highly successful for a wide range of natural language processing tasks, it does have some limitations.

Firstly, it is inherently sequential. Although the transformer architecture is designed to process input sequences in parallel, which can be computationally efficient, it is not naturally suited for tasks that require sequential processing, such as those involving the generation of output sequences step-by-step.

Furthermore, **since transformers do not preserve information about the position of the input sequence, it can be difficult to model certain types of sequential dependencies**. This limitation can be partially overcome by adding positional encoding to the input sequence, but this may still not be sufficient for some tasks. It is also important to remember that the transformer architecture requires a large amount of memory to store attention weights and intermediate representations of the input sequence. This can make it challenging to train on large datasets or use in resource-constrained environments.

In this context, the attention mechanism used in the transformer architecture can be difficult to interpret, which can limit the ability to understand how the model is making predictions. This can be a problem in applications where interpretability is important, such as medical diagnosis or legal decision-making. Although the transformer architecture has shown impressive performance on a wide range of natural language processing tasks, it may not be generalisable to tasks that require knowledge beyond the scope of the training data. For example, a language model trained on news articles may not perform well on medical texts without further specific training.

Overall, while the transformer architecture offers many advantages, it is important to carefully consider its limitations and applicability to specific tasks.

Among other products, BERT (Bidirectional Encoder Representations from Transformers), the Google foundation till 2023 should not be forgotten in term of way to work. Along with GPT (Generative Pre-trained Transformer), both have been large-scale language models based on the Transformer architecture. However, they have some fundamental differences in terms of architecture and training objectives. BERT is a bidirectional model that can consider the context of a word from both the left and right sides. It was pre-trained using a masked language modelling objective, where some of the words in the input text were randomly replaced with a special "mask" token, and the model was trained to predict the original word from the masked context. BERT also used another training objective called next sentence prediction, where the model was trained to predict whether two sentences are contiguous in the input text. This made BERT particularly suitable for tasks that required understanding the context and relationships between different parts of a sentence, such as question answering, natural language inference, and sentiment analysis.

On the other hand, GPT is a unidirectional model that uses an autoregressive language modelling objective, where the model is trained to predict the next word in a sequence given the previous words. This allows GPT to generate coherent and fluent text and has been used for various generation tasks, such as machine translation, text summarisation, and dialogue generation.

In summary, BERT/Gemini and GPT are both powerful language models that utilise the Transformer architecture but have different strengths and objectives. BERT/Gemini is better suited for tasks that require understanding the context and relationships between different parts of a sentence, while GPT/Gemini is more suited for language generation tasks.

In the rapidly evolving field of artificial intelligence, BERT has been replaced by Gemini and in the mean time LLaMA (Large Language Model Meta AI) has reached an high level of performances. Each of these models represents a significant leap forward in natural language processing and generation. We will briefly highlight a comparison of these three AI powerhouses, exploring their origins, capabilities, and potential impacts on various industries.

We have already described GPT approach that is evolving with different levels 3.5, 4o, and progressively 5, that are moving faster ahead compared to the described GPT-3, released in 2020, marked a pivotal moment in AI history with its 175 billion parameters, setting a new standard for large language models.

Gemini, developed by Google AI, was announced in December 2023 as a multimodal AI model. It represents Google's response to the growing demand for more versatile and powerful AI systems. Gemini was designed from the ground up to seamlessly understand and generate various types of data, including text, code, audio, image, and video.

LLaMA, introduced by Meta (formerly Facebook) in 2023, aimed to provide a more efficient and accessible large language model. Unlike its predecessors, LLaMA was released with different sizes (7B, 13B, 33B, and 65B parameters), allowing researchers and developers to choose the most suitable version for their needs.

GPT, Gemini, and LLaMA represent the cutting edge of AI language models, each with its unique strengths and applications. While GPT has set the standard for large language models, Gemini's multimodal approach and LLaMA's focus on efficiency and accessibility are pushing the boundaries of what's possible in AI.

As these technologies continue to develop, they promise to reshape industries and our interaction with digital systems in profound ways.

The future of AI is undoubtedly exciting, but it also calls for careful consideration of the ethical implications and responsible development practices. As we marvel at the capabilities of these AI giants, we must also ensure that their deployment benefits humanity as a whole.

Feature	GPT	Gemini	LLaMA
Language Understanding and Generation	Excels in natural language understanding and generation	Superior performance, especially in multimodal tasks	Strong capabilities, focused on efficiency
Multimodal Abilities	Primarily text-based, some multimodal capabilities in later versions	Designed for multimodal tasks, excels in understanding across different modalities	Primarily text-based, but extensions exist for other modalities
Coding and Technical Tasks	Demonstrates strong coding abilities	Exceptional performance in coding tasks	Capable of coding tasks, but perhaps not as specialized
Accessibility and Deployment	Closed-source, access through APIs	Initially available through Google's AI services, with plans for wider accessibility	Open-source, allowing researchers and developers to freely use and modify
Computational Requirements	Requires significant computational resources	Designed for efficiency, but still requires substantial resources	Offers more flexibility with model sizes, making it more accessible
Ethical Considerations and Biases	Faces challenges related to biases and ethical considerations	Still under evaluation for potential biases	Presents both opportunities for transparency and risks of misuse
Impact on Industries	Potential in healthcare, education, and creative industries	Could revolutionize medical imaging and provide immersive learning experiences	Offers possibilities for more accessible AI integration, especially in resource-constrained environments
Future Prospects	Further improvements in accuracy and reduction of biases, seamless integration into everyday applications, increased focus on ethical AI development	Similar prospects, with a focus on multimodal capabilities and broader accessibility	Similar prospects, with a focus on open-source development and customization

Emerging Contenders: Mistral and Alpha Aleph

While GPT, Gemini, and LLaMA have established themselves as major players in the AI field, two newer models have been gaining attention: Mistral and Alpha Aleph. Let's explore how these emerging contenders compare to the established giants.

Mistral AI, a French startup, introduced its eponymous language model in September 2023. Mistral has quickly gained recognition for its impressive performance despite its relatively small size. Mistral models are notably smaller than many competitors, yet achieve comparable or superior performance on various benchmarks (efficiency). Like LLaMA, Mistral has released open-source versions of its models, fostering innovation and accessibility and offers models optimised for different tasks, including a model specifically designed for coding (Mistral Instruct). Despite its smaller size, Mistral has shown impressive results in language understanding tasks, often outperforming larger models and has demonstrated strong capabilities in code generation and understanding.

Mistral models are significantly smaller than GPT or Gemini, yet offer competitive performance, potentially allowing for more widespread deployment and the open-source approach makes it more accessible to researchers and developers. While not as broadly capable as GPT or Gemini in multimodal tasks, Mistral's specialised models offer strong performance in specific areas like coding.

Alpha Aleph is an advanced AI system developed by LAION (Large-scale Artificial Intelligence Open Network), a non-profit organisation dedicated to making AI more accessible. Built on open-source principles, aiming to democratise access to advanced AI capabilities, being designed to handle various types of data, including text, images, and potentially other modalities it leverages contributions from a global community of researchers and developers. Alpha Aleph aims to compete with commercial models in various language and multimodal tasks and emphasises open-source development, contrasting with the more closed nature of GPT and Gemini. Similar to Gemini, Alpha Aleph is designed with multimodal capabilities in mind, though the extent of these capabilities is still being explored. A characteristic is that Alpha Aleph relies more heavily on community contributions.

In the following table some comparison of these emerging contenders and established AI models.

Feature	Mistral	Alpha Aleph	GPT	Gemini	LLaMA
Size and Efficiency	Smaller than GPT-3 or Gemini, yet competitive performance	Not explicitly mentioned, but likely comparable to larger models	Large scale	Large scale	Smaller scale
Open-Source	Yes	Yes	No	Partially open-source (Gemini)	Yes
Multimodal Capabilities	Primarily text-based, with specialized models for coding	Designed for multimodal tasks	Primarily text-based (with some multimodal capabilities in later versions)	Designed for multimodal tasks	Primarily text-based (with extensions for other modalities)
Community-Driven	To some extent	Strongly emphasized	Corporate-backed	Corporate-backed	Corporate-backed
Specialized Models	Offers specialized models for coding	Not explicitly mentioned	General-purpose	General-purpose	General-purpose
Performance	Impressive language understanding and coding capabilities	Aims to compete with commercial models	Excels in natural language understanding and generation	Superior performance in language tasks, especially multimodal	Strong language understanding and generation capabilities

Impact on the AI Landscape

The emergence of models like Mistral and Alpha Aleph is reshaping the AI landscape:

- **Democratisation of AI:** These models are making advanced AI capabilities more accessible to a wider range of researchers, developers, and organisations.

- **Efficiency focus:** Mistral's success with smaller models is pushing the industry towards more efficient AI systems, potentially reducing computational requirements and environmental impact.

- **Open collaboration:** The open-source nature of these models is fostering a more collaborative AI development ecosystem, potentially accelerating innovation.

- **Ethical considerations:** As more players enter the field, there's an increased focus on developing AI systems with careful consideration of ethical implications and potential biases.

Artificial Intelligence and Quantum Computing

It is important to note that a quantum processing unit (QPU) is a different type of hardware with distinct computational principles. Thanks to its exponentially higher processing capacity compared to a traditional computer, it is an **excellent candidate for developing new machine learning algorithms** based on purely quantum principles. Quantum computing is rapidly emerging in the information technology market, despite being an immature technology with an evolution that is not yet clearly defined. Its disruptive entrance challenges various aspects of the computational world as we know it, requiring different skills compared to those traditionally employed in computer science. The use of quantum mechanics laws necessitates working with hardware technology at temperatures close to absolute zero and structuring programming in an appropriate manner.

Quantum computing offers a fundamentally different, yet complementary approach to traditional computing, radically increasing computational capabilities. The concept of quantum computing was first proposed by Richard Feynman, who argued that by leveraging the effects of quantum mechanics, exponentially faster calculations could be achieved. Instead of further miniaturising silicon technology, as has been done until now, a paradigm shift is being made. The goal is to exploit the properties of atomic particles to encode more information into each state.[6]

In a transistor-based system, at each clock cycle, the state of a single unit, the bit, can only be 0 or 1 (binary system). Without digging into a detailed description, the advantage of quantum computing lies in **utilising two typical conditions of quantum physics: "entanglement" and "superposition."** These phenomena allow the use of quantum particles to define a wide variety of information within a single state, which would correspond to a series of "traditional bits." For example, with a microprocessor containing N bits, it is possible to represent 2^N states (a linear growth). However, with **N qubits (the basic units of a quantum computer), the possibilities are 2 raised to the power of N,** exponentially increasing power and speed, even for extremely complex calculations, effectively reducing processing times from years for a traditional computer to mere minutes for a quantum computer.

Returning to machine learning, one model involves generating classical data with data processing executed on a quantum computer. Thus, data such as text, images, or time series must be converted into a format that a quantum computer can interpret. A quantum computer can only process quantum data, and a quantum algorithm produces outputs that must be converted back into classical data for the next step of the algorithm. Since **converting data** in both directions requires at least a linear time complexity in relation to data size, the speed **advantages may be diminished**.

The scenario is different when the **data is inherently quantum, a common situation in departments of physics, chemistry, or biology**. The electrons of the quantum CPU or the molecules in pharmaceuticals comply with the laws of quantum mechanics. By using quantum data to simulate quantum particles, we could run "quantum machine learning" algorithms directly on this type of data. The theoretical advantages in this case are considerable.

Currently, several **hybrid quantum-classical architectures** have been proposed and utilised, where models are distributed between classical and quantum processing units. This allows quantum data processing on a computer while taking advantage of well-understood computations on classical computers. For instance, classical computers can be used to optimise outer loops for quantum neural networks. An example of this is TensorFlow Quantum, a library for hybrid quantum-classical machine learning used by Google, primarily aimed at applications involving the generation of quantum data but also used for classical data. A practical example implementing this principle is a simplified **quantum convolutional neural network (QCNN)**, a quantum analogue of a classical convolutional neural network that is also translationally invariant.

---

[6] J. D. Hidary "Quantum Computing: An Applied Approach" Springer, 2021

To provide a concrete example of the described hybrid model, we can cite the last year announcement of a collaboration between IBM and Moderna to leverage AI and quantum computing technologies to advance research on mRNA models. In this collaboration, Moderna will use the AI capabilities of IBM Research and generative model technologies for the design and optimisation of mRNA drugs. This opens up a new frontier in the life sciences where the ethical use of two cutting-edge technologies could bring immeasurable benefits to humanity.

But we can't remain on this point because there are some additional evaluations and perspectives on the interplay between AI and quantum computing that could enrich the analysis.

AI and quantum computing (QC) are not just complementary technologies but could potentially enhance each other's development. Quantum algorithms, such as those leveraging quantum parallelism, could accelerate machine learning tasks that are currently limited by classical computational speeds. Conversely, AI techniques could be used to optimise quantum algorithms and manage quantum noise, which is a significant challenge in the current generation of quantum computers. This bidirectional influence could lead to rapid advancements in both fields.

While the theoretical potential of combining AI with QC is immense, **practical limitations still exist.** Quantum computers are currently in their nascent stages, with issues related to qubit coherence, error rates, and the need for extremely low temperatures to maintain quantum states. AI models that require substantial quantum computational resources may not yet see significant gains due to these hardware constraints. This gap highlights the importance of continued investment in quantum hardware development alongside software and algorithmic innovations.

Before we have touched on the challenges of converting classical data into quantum data and vice versa, which could limit speed advantages. This process is not just computationally intensive but also fundamentally challenging, as it requires rethinking how data is represented and processed. Future research could focus on developing more efficient data encoding schemes for quantum computing or hybrid approaches that minimise the need for data conversion, thereby reducing the overhead and preserving the computational advantages of quantum systems.

QC could potentially revolutionise existing machine learning paradigms by introducing new quantum-based models and algorithms. For example, quantum neural networks could operate on principles different from classical networks, potentially allowing for faster training and more efficient data processing. This could also lead to entirely new types of learning models that leverage quantum phenomena such as entanglement and superposition. Exploring these new paradigms could open up avenues for breakthroughs in fields like natural language processing, computer vision, and beyond.

The successful integration of AI and QC will likely require close collaboration between computer scientists, quantum physicists, and domain experts from fields like chemistry and biology. The development of quantum machine learning algorithms that directly process quantum data from these disciplines could lead to new discoveries and applications that were previously unattainable. This collaborative approach is crucial for overcoming the technical challenges and realising the full potential of quantum-enhanced AI.

As with any advanced technology, the convergence of AI and quantum computing raises ethical considerations. These technologies could be used to solve complex problems in drug discovery, cryptography, and climate modelling, but they also pose risks related to data privacy, security, and the potential for misuse. We will se that is vital to address these concerns proactively by establishing ethical guidelines and ensuring that these technologies are developed with a focus on societal benefit.

The race to develop quantum computing capabilities is not just a technological challenge but also an economic and strategic one. Countries and companies that lead in quantum computing and AI will have a significant advantage in various industries, from pharmaceuticals to finance. This potential for a strategic edge adds another layer of importance to investments in quantum-AI research and development, and it is something policymakers and business leaders must consider.

For quantum computing to become a mainstream tool for AI, significant advancements in scalability and error correction are needed. Current quantum devices are often referred to as Noisy Intermediate-Scale Quantum (NISQ) devices, which limits their application. To fully harness the power of quantum computing in AI, major players are developing their own roadmap for developing fault-tolerant quantum computers. Research should also focus on creating hybrid algorithms that make the best use of both quantum and classical computing resources, maximising efficiency while hardware capabilities catch up.[7]

Looking forward, quantum computing could enable the development of AI models that are currently infeasible due to computational constraints. These could include models that simulate extremely complex systems, such as entire ecosystems, or models that provide real-time adaptive solutions in highly dynamic environments. Such advancements could redefine the limits of what AI can achieve and expand its applications to new, unexplored areas.

---

[7] Conference Paper "Quantum Computing's Path to Supremacy: Progress in the NISQ Epoch" Springer Link, 2024

All the above highlight what is the major weakness in background, the integration of AI and quantum computing will also require a new generation of talent equipped with knowledge in both fields. Educational initiatives and interdisciplinary training programs will be essential to prepare the workforce to handle the challenges and opportunities presented by these technologies. There is a need to cultivate expertise not just in quantum physics or computer science alone, but at their intersection with AI, data science, and domain-specific knowledge.

Huge challenges and broader implication lay lie ahead to make the evolution viable and beneficial.

The landscape

The AI landscape is rapidly evolving, with new models like Mistral and Alpha Aleph challenging the dominance of established players like GPT, Gemini, and LLaMA. This competition is driving innovation in efficiency, accessibility, and capabilities, ultimately benefiting users and developers alike.

As these models continue to develop, we can expect further advancements in natural language processing, multimodal understanding, and AI applications across various industries. The emphasis on open-source development and efficiency seen in newer models may also lead to more widespread adoption of AI technologies in diverse settings.

However, as the field grows more complex, it becomes increasingly important to consider the ethical implications and potential societal impacts of these powerful AI systems. The future of AI looks promising, but it requires careful navigation to ensure that these advancements benefit humanity as a whole.

Part Two - AI in everyday jobs

Chapter 4
Artificial Intelligence in Professions

A recent Goldman Sachs study attempted to identify and estimate the sectors where job roles will be most influenced, and in some cases profoundly challenged, by the presence of Artificial Intelligence. Among these are administrative professions (48 percent), legal professions (44 percent), architecture and engineering (37 percent), business and financial professions (35 percent), and even management (32 percent) and sales (31 percent).[8]

However, for those who fear that this will lead to job elimination, it should be noted that this should not result in a "negative balance" of jobs, but generally involves a transformation of roles. This, however, requires growth and change in skills that will demand a higher level of abstraction, design, and collaboration within organisations and along supply chains. The real competition, in fact, is not from Artificial Intelligence itself, but from those workers and professionals who make the best use of it. That is confirmed also by recent studies have refined these estimates. For instance, a 2023 report by the International Labour Organisation (ILO) suggests that while AI will affect most jobs, its impact will be more nuanced. The report indicates that about 27% of tasks across occupations could be automated, but complete job displacement is less likely than task transformation.

In fact as AI adoption increases, new roles are emerging. For example, "AI ethicists" and "AI-human collaboration specialists" are becoming crucial in organisations implementing AI systems. We will see in a following chapter that these roles focus on ensuring ethical AI use and optimising human-AI interaction. On this point the World Economic Forum's "Future of Jobs Report 2023" emphasises the growing importance of skills like analytical thinking, creative thinking, and AI literacy across industries. This confirms the original point about the need for higher-level skills.

Entering the Sector-Specific Developments a lot of attention regards the Legal Sector whereAI tools like contract analysis software and predictive justice algorithms are becoming prevalent in some country, changing how legal professionals work rather than replacing them entirely.

---

[8] Goldman Sachs "AI is showing "very positive" signs of eventually boosting GDP and productivity" 2024

Financial Services as been one of the first embracing the AI techniques since years being increasingly used for fraud detection, algorithmic trading, and personalised financial advice, requiring finance professionals to adapt and leverage these tools.

Another area is Healthcare that is seeing significant AI integration, with applications in diagnostics, treatment planning, and drug discovery.

In response to these changes, many countries and organisations are launching initiatives to re-skill and up-skill workers, in some case with dedicated funding like in the case of the European Union's Digital Europe Programme.

As AI's influence grows, so does the need for regulation. The EU's AI Act and similar initiatives worldwide are shaping how AI can be used in professional settings, adding another layer of complexity to its integration in various sectors. In this scenario Small and Medium Enterprises (SMEs) are also increasingly finding ways to leverage AI tools.

We can say though that the impact of the technology n professions continues to evolve rapidly. While the original Goldman Sachs estimates provide a useful baseline, the reality is proving to be more nuanced. The key to thriving in this AI-enhanced professional landscape lies in continuous learning, adaptability, and the strategic use of AI as a tool to augment human capabilities rather than replace them. As AI technologies become more sophisticated and accessible, the distinction between "AI-using" and "non-AI-using" professionals within the same field is likely to become a significant factor in career advancement and competitiveness.

AI in Civil Engineering and Architecture: Revolutionising the Construction Industry

Artificial Intelligence (AI) is transforming the civil engineering sector, enhancing the efficiency of infrastructure projects and spearheading the digital revolution in construction. Let's explore some key applications and recent developments, with a particular focus on the European landscape.

BIM AND AI: A POWERFUL SYNERGY

Building Information Modelling (BIM) has become increasingly prevalent in civil engineering projects. When combined with AI, it creates a powerful tool for design optimisation. Through dedicated APIs, AI can learn to replicate repetitive tasks error-free, freeing up design capacity for higher-value aspects of projects.

European firms are at the forefront of this integration. For instance, Arup, a UK-based firm, has developed an AI-powered BIM tool that can generate and evaluate multiple design options based on specified parameters, significantly reducing design time and improving outcomes.

Intelligent Design and Analysis

AI-powered applications are emerging that can automatically extract and analyse data necessary for design (material properties, energy data, environmental characteristics, etc.). These tools can propose solutions to complex architectural challenges, fostering intelligent design from the initial draft.

In the Netherlands, the company MVRDV has utilised AI in their "Porocity" project, creating urban designs that optimise for factors like sunlight, air quality, and traffic flow simultaneously.

PROJECT MANAGEMENT AND RISK MITIGATION

Machine learning algorithms provide clearer cost estimates and more accurate budgets based on previous project results and future predictions. AI can also plan project timelines, accounting for potential risks.

European construction giant Vinci has implemented AI-driven project management tools that have reportedly reduced project overruns by 15% across their portfolio basically **Improving forecasting accuracy** predicting project costs and timelines. During the execution it was possible to **Enhance risk management,** proactively identifying and mitigating risks. Overall the application **optimises the resource allocation.** That fosters **innovation** facilitating new ways to improve project delivery and reduce costs.

Over the time analysing past projects and identifying correlation between weather delays and specific construction phases, allows to incorporate contingency plans for weather-related disruptions into future projects, significantly reducing project overruns.

CONSTRUCTION PROCESS MANAGEMENT

AI-powered robots equipped with cameras can autonomously move through construction sites, acquiring 3D Images. Neural networks compare these images with BIM model data to track project progress. In Sweden, the startup Spotscale uses AI and drone technology to create highly accurate 3D models of construction sites, enabling real-time progress monitoring and deviation detection.

3D PRINTING AND ROBOTICS

AI-based 3D printing technology allows for the automation of much of the construction process, enabling the "printing" of large structures and 3D objects at high speed and with great precision. The Dutch company MX3D has successfully 3D printed a steel bridge in Amsterdam using AI-guided robots, showcasing the potential of this technology in civil engineering.

SAFETY AND RISK MANAGEMENT

AI can identify potential hazards in the construction process and implement risk control measures. AI-enabled cameras and networks can constantly monitor all areas of the site, assessing equipment usage, tracking progress, and analysing activities in real time. The European Union's "Construction 4.0" initiative is promoting the use of AI for safety management across member states, with pilot projects showing promising results in reducing workplace accidents.

STRUCTURAL HEALTH MONITORING

Intelligent systems can monitor the health of buildings and large-scale infrastructure projects like bridges, pipelines, and dams. Smart sensors enable periodic measurements and continuous surveillance strategies to assess structural vulnerability and maintain high levels of safety and efficiency over time. In Italy, the University of Padua has developed an AI system that monitors the structural health of Venice's historic buildings, helping preserve the city's architectural heritage while ensuring public safety.

FACILITY MANAGEMENT

After project completion, facility managers can rely on AI to monitor energy consumption, optimise plant performance, schedule predictive maintenance, and improve health and safety protocols. These applications are made possible by integrating AI with Internet of Things (IoT) technologies and smart sensors throughout the structure. The Paris-based company Energisme has developed an AI platform that optimises energy consumption in commercial buildings, resulting in up to 30% energy savings for its clients.

FUTURE PROSPECTS

As AI continues to evolve, it promises to enable the management of buildings and building complexes while considering all historical and surrounding data, a feat currently challenging to achieve. This holistic approach will lead to more sustainable, efficient, and resilient infrastructure. The European Commission's "Horizon Europe" program is actively funding research into AI applications in civil engineering, aiming to position Europe as a global leader in smart construction technologies.

In conclusion, AI is proving to be a valuable ally for all those involved in the design, construction, and management of civil works. It allows for better project planning, optimal design solutions, improved cost and time control, increased efficiency and productivity, and enhanced safety measures. As these technologies continue to advance, we can look forward to smarter, more sustainable cities and infrastructure across Europe and beyond.

AI in Sustainable Building Design and European Infrastructure Projects

Artificial Intelligence is revolutionising sustainable building design by optimising energy efficiency, material usage, and overall environmental impact. Here are some key applications:

1. Energy Optimisation

AI algorithms can analyse vast amounts of data to optimise building energy consumption. The Dutch company Deerns uses AI to design smart building systems that continuously adjust heating, cooling, and lighting based on occupancy patterns and weather forecasts, reducing energy consumption by up to 30%. In Germany, Siemens' AI-driven building management system, Desigo CC, integrates with renewable energy sources to maximise clean energy usage and minimise reliance on the grid.

2. Material Selection and Circular Economy

AI is helping architects and engineers choose sustainable materials and design for circularity: The UK-based company Topolytics uses AI to track construction waste and identify opportunities for material reuse, supporting circular economy principles in construction. In Sweden, AI startup Spacemaker helps architects optimise building designs for minimal material waste while maximising natural light and energy efficiency.

3. Biophilic Design

AI is being used to incorporate nature-inspired elements into building design. Foster & Partners, a British architectural firm, uses AI algorithms to optimise building facades for plant growth, creating "living buildings" that improve air quality and biodiversity in urban environments.

4. AI in Major European Infrastructure Projects

AI-powered 'digital twins' were used to simulate and optimise the construction process, reducing delays and cost overruns. Machine learning algorithms analysed sensor data from tunnelling machines to predict and prevent equipment failures, improving safety and efficiency. We should mention also Porto Metro Extension, in Portugal where the ongoing expansion of Porto's metro system leverages AI for optimising tunnel boring machine operations using predictive maintenance algorithms and keep a real-time monitoring of ground movement during construction, with AI analysing data from thousands of sensors to prevent subsidence. Also Stockholm Bypass Project, in Sweden used traffic flow optimisation during construction, with AI models predicting and mitigating congestion registering and environmental impact reduction, using AI to model and minimise noise and air pollution from construction activities. Last but not least the HS2 High-Speed Rail, in UK connecting London to northern England, incorporates AI in various ways starting from AI-driven design optimisation for noise barriers, reducing community impact and through an automated vegetation mapping along the route using machine learning and satellite imagery, aiding in biodiversity preservation efforts.

We may add several other examples of AI already extensively used for design, construction phase and life monitoring of important infrastructures.

The **emerging trends** and future prospects are among progressively projects using **AI-powered digital twins** of buildings and infrastructure allowing for real-time optimisation and predictive maintenance.

Important effect also to model and optimise urban development, considering factors like air quality, traffic flow, and quality of life, **influencing urban planning** considering factors like air quality, traffic flow, and quality of life, like in done in Barcelona.

Another aspect to consider is the adaptation to changing climate conditions over their lifespan and that may require new ways to model.

Research is ongoing into fully autonomous construction processes, with AI coordinating **robots and 3D printing** technologies, influencing also **the development of new, sustainable building materials** by simulating material properties and optimising compositions.

As these technologies continue to evolve, we can expect even more innovative applications of AI in sustainable building design and infrastructure projects across Europe. The integration of AI not only improves efficiency and sustainability but also opens up new possibilities for creating smarter, more resilient built environments.

The most pressing challenge is to ensure consistent, transnational AI training for all employees. This is essential to mitigate risks associated with accountability, transparency, and fairness that can occur when AI is implemented haphazardly. A uniform approach is vital for organisations operating across Europe.

Beyond construction management and satellite image analysis for land use monitoring, AI can identify changes in land cover, such as urban expansion and deforestation. This data is crucial for infrastructure planning and natural disaster risk assessment.

AI is also revolutionising **intelligent transportation systems,** optimising traffic and public transport through data analysis and route optimisation.

While challenges like high implementation costs and the need for specialised AI systems persist, the potential of AI to transform the construction industry is undeniable. In the energy sector, AI is streamlining the management of **complex power grids**. With thousands of kilometres of high-voltage lines and hundreds of substations, the Italian grid benefits from AI-powered remote monitoring and predictive maintenance. Digital twins of the electrical grid are enabling more accurate modelling and forecasting.

To effectively utilise AI in engineering and architecture, professionals should possess a foundational understanding of AI concepts like machine learning and data modelling. **Data analysis** skills, **programming** abilities (especially Python and R),and knowledge of sensor technologies, robotics, and drones are also essential.

Tools like ChatGPT are being explored for generating design options and automating routine tasks in architecture and engineering.

The **Reinforcement Learning technique** is being used to optimise construction processes, such as scheduling and resource allocation to cope with the already mentioned Building Information Modelling (**BIM**). The possibility to accelerate the discovery of new materials with specific properties for construction may drive to design **sustainability** optimising energy consumption.

As AI becomes more integrated into engineering, it is essential to address ethical concerns such as bias, transparency, and accountability. **Protecting sensitive data** is paramount, especially when dealing with personal information or proprietary business data.

Successful AI implementation often requires **collaboration** between engineers, data scientists, and domain experts.

The intersection of AI and engineering is evolving rapidly. As AI technologies continue to advance, their applications in the construction industry will become increasingly sophisticated, driving innovation and efficiency. By understanding the fundamentals of AI and staying abreast of the latest developments, engineers can leverage these powerful tools to create more sustainable, resilient, and intelligent built environments.

Industrial Vision Systems and AI Applications

Machine vision, alongside end-effectors (devices attached to the robot/cobot wrist that enable interaction with the environment), is a crucial element in industrial technologies utilising AI. Through AI-powered vision systems, machines in general, and robots in particular, acquire the capabilities to "see", "understand", and "interpret", which are necessary to perform their assigned tasks and interact with human operators.

CURRENT APPLICATIONS

Numerous applications of AI vision systems associated with collaborative robots (co-bots) are already in use in industrial settings. Once a neural network is trained to recognise a good image based on a series of labelled examples, it can automatically distinguish between a good component and a defective one, considering expected variations. As the system classifies more images, it becomes increasingly precise and reliable, refining its classification and, consequently, its inspection capabilities.[9]

We list just some Key Applications:

- **Recognition**: Robots equipped with machine vision perform quality control by recognising manufacturing defects or deviations from standard characteristics (e.g., in the agri-food industry). The advantages in these tasks include:
    - Precision unattainable by the human eye
    - Co-bots' immunity to distractions in repetitive processes
    - Establishment of objective and repeatable criteria
    - Ability to involve human supervisors when the machine cannot make a decision

- **Orientation, Positioning, and Guidance**: These operations are generally associated with pallet movement and loading management. Vision sensors guide the robot's anthropomorphic arm by recognising the position and orientation of objects to be grasped (e.g., cardboard boxes) and the space in which to deposit them, also considering the potential presence of other moving objects or people.

- **Non-contact Measurements:** Any type of measurement unit – length, width, diameter, volume, etc. – can potentially be estimated without contact through AI vision systems. This offers clear advantages in environments where human intervention would jeopardise the psychophysical integrity of the operator (steel industry) or the products (fragile objects).

- **Verification:** This is an extension of recognition applied to conveyor belts or metal sheets, for example, when checking for processing defects on metal sheets or in textile production.

- **Classification and Selection:** This is one of the most complex operations that a co=bot with machine vision can perform. For instance, choosing between objects of different nature, grasping them, and repositioning them based on classification. Vision systems can also recognise and classify the

---

[9]A. Khang, V. A. Hajimahmud, A. Misra, E. Litvinova "Machine Vision and Industrial Robotics in Manufacturing: Approaches, Technologies, and Applications" CRC Press, 2024

various postures in which the same object may be randomly arranged, thus estimating optimal grasping points.

- **Reading:** This is a typical application that follows packaging and precedes boxing or pallet loading: recognising a package, checking its barcode, grasping the object, inserting it into a box, or positioning it on a pallet.

- **Counting:** Machine vision systems can count a specific number of objects (e.g., the number of screws in a package) or the number of occurrences of a feature in a particular object (e.g., components on a printed circuit board).

- **Surveillance and Interaction**: This application has the most implications for safety in human-machine interaction within the same work environment. Artificial vision systems recognise the position and movement of operators and provide co=bots with the necessary information to interact with them without making contact.

In the context of industrial vision systems, **both non-generative and generative AI techniques are employed**, each with its own strengths and applications.

Non-generative AI, which includes traditional machine learning and deep learning techniques, is primarily used for tasks such as classification, detection, and prediction based on existing data. In industrial vision systems, non-generative AI is commonly used for:

- Image Classification: Identifying and categorising objects or defects in images.

- Object Detection: Locating and identifying multiple objects within an image.

- Semantic Segmentation: Partitioning an image into semantically meaningful parts.

- Anomaly Detection: Identifying unusual patterns that do not conform to expected behaviour.

These techniques rely on supervised or unsupervised learning from large datasets of labelled or unlabelled images. Convolutional Neural Networks (CNNs) are a popular architecture for many of these tasks due to their ability to learn hierarchical features from

Generative AI, on the other hand, can create new data instances that resemble the training data. In industrial vision systems, generative AI is beginning to find applications in:

- Data Augmentation: Generating synthetic images to expand training datasets, especially useful for rare defect cases.

- Anomaly Detection: Using techniques like Generative Adversarial Networks (GANs) to learn the distribution of normal data and identify anomalies.

- <u>Image-to-Image Translation:</u> Converting images from one domain to another, which can be useful for simulating different lighting conditions or wear patterns.
- <u>Super-Resolution</u>: Enhancing the resolution of low-quality images for better inspection.

The difference-maker in all the listed applications is the ability of vision systems to learn through Machine Learning or Deep Learning, progressively improving and optimising processes.

- <u>Machine Learning</u>: Traditional machine learning algorithms like Support Vector Machines (SVMs) and Random Forests are still used for simpler classification tasks and when interpretability is crucial.
- <u>Deep Learning</u>: Deep learning models, particularly CNNs, have become the go-to solution for most complex vision tasks due to their ability to automatically learn hierarchical features from raw pixel data.
- <u>Transfer Learning:</u> This technique allows the adaptation of pre-trained models to specific industrial tasks, reducing the need for large, domain-specific datasets.
- <u>Reinforcement Learning</u>: Increasingly used in robotic control and path planning, enabling co-bots to learn optimal strategies for interacting with their environment.
- <u>Few-Shot Learning:</u> This approach is gaining traction in industrial settings where obtaining large labelled datasets is challenging, allowing models to learn from a small number of examples.

Recent Advancements with **Transformers and other attention-based architectures are being adapted** for vision tasks, offering improved performance on complex scene understanding problems, enabling more efficient use of unlabelled data, which is often abundant in industrial settings. It increases, there's a **growing focus on developing interpretable models** that can explain their decisions, crucial for quality control and regulatory compliance.

In addition the deployment of AI models directly on edge devices is enabling real-time processing and reducing latency in industrial vision systems including point cloud processing and 3D object detection, expanding the capabilities of industrial robots in complex environments.

By leveraging these advanced AI techniques, industrial vision systems are becoming more adaptive, efficient, and capable of handling increasingly complex tasks in dynamic manufacturing environments.

A lot of debates on **humanoid robots**, designed to resemble and mimic human form and behaviour, have long captured the imagination of both the public and industry. In industrial settings, the application of humanoid robots presents both exciting possibilities and significant challenges.

In **assembly and manufacturing**, i.e. fine motor tasks in electronics assembly as well as collaborative work in automotive manufacturing and flexible production lines with frequent changeovers, humanoid robots can potentially use the same tools and operate in the same spaces designed for human workers, reducing the need for specialised equipment. It is the case of Honda's ASIMO, has demonstrated capabilities in fine motor control that could be applicable in assembly tasks. It is a debatable topic considering the potential job loss coming with these solutions.

No debate instead for **hazardous environment operations** as nuclear plant maintenance and decommissioning or chemical spill clean-up as well as deep-sea operations, Humanoid form allows these robots to navigate environments designed for humans while keeping human workers safe from harm as NASA's Valkyrie robot is being developed for potential use in disaster response scenarios.

The humanoid form **serves also as an ideal platform for developing** technologies that can later be applied to more specialised robots or exoskeletons.

We can't hide the limitations for this approach, humanoid robots are generally **more expensive** than specialised industrial robots due to their complexity and for many tasks, **purpose-built robots or traditional industrial arms are more efficient and reliable.** Maintaining **balance while performing tasks** is a significant challenge for bipedal robots and **the energy required to operate** a full humanoid body is often impractical for long-term industrial use and the complex mechanisms required for humanoid movement are often **less durable than simpler, task-specific designs.**

The idea of **humanoid robots seamlessly replacing human** workers across various industries **remains largely in the realm of science fiction.** Humanoid robots with human-like emotional intelligence and decision-making capabilities are still far from reality and the concept of robots indistinguishable from humans in appearance and behaviour is not currently viable for industrial applications.

Rather than replacing humans entirely, humanoid robots are more likely to find niches where they can complement human workers, in fact many current humanoid robots in industry are at least partially tele-operated, rather than fully autonomous so they are likely to remain limited to specific use cases where their form factor provides a clear advantage over other designs.

While fully autonomous, multi-purpose humanoid robots in industry **remain a distant goal**, advancements in several key areas could increase their viability and that require to enhance the adaptability and decision-making capabilities, lighter, stronger materials, advancements in battery technology and more sophisticated control systems could improve balance and fine motor control, making humanoids more practical for a wider range of tasks.

While humanoid robots have made significant strides and found some niche applications in industrial environments, **their widespread adoption faces substantial technical and economic challenges.** The future of humanoid robots in industry likely lies in specialised applications where their human-like form provides distinct advantages, rather than as universal replacements for human workers. As technology advances, the line between futuristic imagery and practical reality may continue to blur, but for the foreseeable future, the role of humanoid robots in industry will remain limited and highly specialised.

Actually, when we're designing AI systems, it makes more sense to think about creating an environment that works well with the technology, rather than trying to make machines look and act exactly like humans – unless there's a really good reason to do so. For example, in some vineyards and farms, the trees and plants are planted at specific heights and distances to make it easier for robots to work without needing complicated arms and hands. This idea of changing the environment to fit the technology is already common in factories, where robots have been used for many years.

AI in the Legal and Judicial World: A European Perspective

Artificial Intelligence (AI) has been part of the legal field for some time now. It has evolved from lawyers using it to quickly review mountains of documents and search for case analogies to much more articulated uses. The arrival of LLM, with its ability to converse in a human-like manner, has opened up unexpected frontiers.

One of the first AI applications in law was **Technology-Assisted Review (TAR)**, also known as predictive coding and computer-assisted review. This approach allows **lawyers to examine a sample of documents**, classifying them according to criteria of interest, and then provide instructions to the machine on how to identify them in the complete dataset. These machine learning systems progressively improve their analyses, significantly lightening the workload in law firms and drastically reducing the time and costs of preliminary document reviews.

In the Anglo-Saxon world, Judge Andrew Peck promoted the use of this methodology in US courts for document review as early as 2012. Today, it forms the basis of many legal research tools used by lawyers across Europe.

AI-powered programs can now provide litigants with a **prediction of case outcomes based on past judgments and judges' behaviours.** This technology is being adopted across Europe, i.e., in France, the startup Case Law Analytics uses machine learning to predict judicial decisions in various areas of law as well as the Estonian Ministry of Justice is developing an AI-powered "robot judge" to adjudicate small claims disputes, aiming to clear case backlogs.

AI is powering many existing legal support products that **automate invoice generation, payment reminders, conflict checks, and client onboarding** activities. Law firms across Europe are adopting these technologies to streamline operations. Just to mention some the UK-based firm Clifford Chance has implemented AI-driven systems for due diligence and contract analysis and in Germany, KPMG Law is using AI for automated document review and contract management.

AI systems can now **create statements or contracts by simply filling in form fields**. The AI system automatically generates a document from a library of intelligent templates created in line with local laws and constantly updated based on official information.

Contract Lifecycle Management (CLM) products use AI to help manage all aspects of contractual relationships between companies. They can create contract drafts with relevant standard clauses for a particular client and scan proposed contracts to compare clauses with standard ones.

AI is making inroads into European judicial systems, for example in Italy, the Court of Cassation has partnered with the University of Pavia to develop AI systems for **jurisprudence and legislation analysis** and at the same time the European Court of Human Rights has implemented a system called **COMPASS to help prioritise cases**. From a **citizens point of view** in the Netherlands, the Rechtwijzer platform uses AI to **guide them through legal procedures and dispute resolution.**

As AI becomes more prevalent in legal systems, there's a growing focus on ethical considerations and the need for explainable AI, for this reason the European Commission for the Efficiency of Justice (CEPEJ) has adopted the European Ethical Charter on the Use of AI in Judicial Systems, providing **guidelines for the responsible use of AI in law**. To be highlights also projects like "Predictive Justice" at the Sant'Anna School of Advanced Studies in Pisa aim to develop **explainable AI systems for legal reasoning.**

As AI continues to transform the legal landscape across Europe, there's an urgent need for lawyers to expand their competence in AI utilisation from an international perspective with the increasing globalisation of legal services, lawyers need to understand how AI is being used in different jurisdictions. The just released EU AI Act will have significant implications for the use of AI in legal contexts across member states. **Lawyers need to be well-versed in these regulations**. As AI systems become more prevalent in law, understanding the ethical implications and potential biases is crucial for lawyers operating in an international context. With AI powering legal research tools across different jurisdictions, it is necessary Ito be proficient in using these tools to provide comprehensive, internationally-informed advice.

Understanding the intersection of AI and data protection laws (like GDPR) is crucial dealing with international clients or cases, as AI-powered arbitration and mediation tools become more common, it is due to understand their operation and implications across different legal systems.

Law firms that can effectively leverage AI in an international context will have a significant competitive advantage in the global legal market. to address these needs, law schools and continuing legal education programs across Europe are beginning to incorporate AI and legal technology into their curricula. As AI continues to evolve and reshape the legal landscape, it's clear that the entire judicial organisation must adapt and expand skillset to include a robust understanding of AI and its applications in law on a European and global scale.

As technology continues to transform the legal landscape, its effects are rippling through legal education and reshaping the future of law practice across Europe. This shift is prompting a reevaluation of traditional legal curricula and forcing law firms to adapt their practices to remain competitive in an increasingly tech-driven industry.

Impact on Legal Education concerns curriculum overhaul from the University inducing not only the knowledge of the new regulation but increasingly **collaborating with computer science** and data science departments:

Legal education is becoming more practice-oriented, with a focus on technology skills an increased focus on teaching the ethical implications of AI in law. to prepare for this AI-driven future, stakeholders in the European legal sector need to take several proactive steps starting from Law Schools and Bar associations and ultimately law firms need to plan investments in AI technologies and training for their staff.

It si a complex process and regulatory bodies must work on creating regulatory frameworks that balance innovation with ethical considerations and public interest, but that is **worthless without individual lawyers committing to lifelong learning** to stay abreast of AI developments and their impact on legal practice. The integration of AI into legal education and practice in Europe is not just a technological shift, but a cultural one. It requires a reimagining of what it means to be a lawyer in the 21st century. As AI continues to evolve, so too will the legal profession, presenting both challenges and opportunities for those willing to adapt and innovate.

AI in the Tax Sector

AI tools are increasingly being used to **automate tasks such as invoicing, accounting, and tax filing**. For years, software has been assisting with the recording of transactions, the generation of reports, and the preparation of financial statements. This now includes electronic invoicing tools that enable the secure sending and receiving of e-invoices in compliance with Italian tax regulations, alongside long-established tax declaration software.

In this context, AI can further streamline document scanning, data classification, and trend identification. Additionally, Robotic Process Automation (RPA) technologies are automating tasks such as opening emails, inputting data, and completing forms autonomously.

These solutions save time, allowing professionals to focus on strategic and value-added activities. They also reduce the risk of human error, ensuring higher accuracy across various stages of automation, which typically leads to better compliance with Italian tax regulations.

Overall, **client service improves**. A key area of interest is Natural Language Processing (NLP), which facilitates the interaction between computers and human language. NLP is being increasingly adopted not only for document management but also for trend identification and report generation. Another growing field is computer vision, which allows the processing of unstructured data, such as graphics and handwritten documents, something that was nearly impossible to automate just a decade ago.

These activities occur within a networked environment that includes tax professionals, certified assistance centres (CAF), and the Italian Revenue Agency. This indicates that beyond the direct benefits to professional practices, system-wide advantages in terms of speed and precision will bring gains to clients and the broader economy alike.

AI tools can also analyse large data sets, identifying trends and opportunities that may be invisible to humans. This helps professionals make better decisions for their clients and discover new ways to enhance their services.

France	Up to 50% of corporate fraud investigations
Italy	Use of big data and AI for risk assessment
Germany	Use of AI for VAT fraud analysis

Fig 1 ch. 4 - use of AI by some EU tax authority

The above table (Figure 1, Chapter 4)[10],[11],[12] shows the area of utilisation of AI-driven data analysis techniques used in the tax sector between 2018 and 2022 in the France, Italy, and Germany. There is a growing trend across all countries, driven by the increasing sophistication of AI, which can quickly and efficiently process large data volumes. However, the percentage remains relatively low, as AI is still a new technology, and professionals and authorities in these countries are still developing the necessary skills to leverage it effectively. The adoption rate is expected to rise as new applications based on machine learning and generative AI become more common.

As seen in Table 2 (Fig. 2, Ch. 4), the use of AI tools for verifying compliance with tax and accounting regulations has increased in the UK, France, Spain, Italy, and Germany between 2018 and 2022. The growing complexity of regulations, combined with the need to reduce costs and the availability of more advanced tools, explains this upward trend.

The main benefits are **improved accuracy** and time savings for both professionals and their clients. By enhancing compliance efficiency, AI helps businesses identify and mitigate the risk of penalties, a factor that justifies the rising adoption rate of AI tools.

---

[10] H. Thompson, "How French tax officials are using AI to track fraud", The Connections, 2023

[11] N. Basic *"Tax audits using artificial intelligence in Italy"* Fiscal Solutions, 2024

[12] T. Wischmeyer, T. Rademacher *"Regulating Artificial Intelligence" Springler Link eBook, 2020*

Year	United Kingdom	France	Spain	Italy	Germany
2016	Initial AI Lab development	-	-	-	-
2020	AI-based fraud detection	-	-	-	-
2021	-	Introduction of AI in audits	-	-	-
2022	-	-	Use of AI for risk assessment	Use of big data and AI for risk assessment	-
2023	-	Up to 50% of corporate fraud investigations	-	Use of AI for VAT fraud analysis	Use of AI for VAT fraud analysis

Fig 2 Ch 4- Milestones of AI for tax compliance verification

Automation of repetitive tasks **can significantly boost efficiency** and reduce costs. Table 3 (Figure 3, Chapter 4) illustrates the increasing use of AI tools to enhance efficiency in tax practices across the UK, France, Spain, Italy, and Germany over recent years. Here too, a consistent upward trend is observed across all nations.

As overall observations we may say that all countries show a steady increase in AI tool adoption over the years, with UK and Germany leading in adoption rates. The most rapid growth seems to occur between 2020 and 2023, possibly due to increased digitalisation during and after the COVID-1 pandemic.

As overall observations we may say that all countries show a steady increase in AI tool adoption over the years, with UK and Germany leading in adoption rates. The most rapid growth seems to occur between 2020 and 2023, possibly due to increased digitalisation during and after the COVID-19 pandemic.

Year	UK	France	Spain	Italy	Germany
2018	15%	12%	10%	8%	14%
2019	20%	16%	13%	11%	18%
2020	28%	22%	18%	15%	25%
2021	35%	30%	25%	22%	32%
2022	45%	40%	35%	30%	42%
2023	55%	52%	48%	42%	54%
2024	65%	62%	58%	55%	64%

Fig 3 Ch. 4 -AI Tool Adoption in Tax Practices (2018-2024)

Note: Percentages represent estimated adoption rates of AI tools in tax practices and are for illustrative purposes only

A specific mention should be made of **chatbots, AI-powered systems designed to simulate human conversations.** Leveraging AI and machine learning, chatbots can respond to customer or user queries in real-time, providing information and guiding users through various processes. This includes tasks like answering frequently asked questions about taxes and accounting, generating documents, and managing tax deadlines. These systems are evolving rapidly, becoming progressively better at understanding natural language and learning from past interactions. Virtual assistants will soon become ubiquitous in the sector, offering opportunities to improve operational efficiency. In addition to the functionalities already discussed, chatbots can assist in creating business plans or helping clients interact with firms, providing real-time information.

Tax authorities are also adopting AI tools for **audit activities**. Table 4 (Figure 4, Chapter 4) shows the percentage of tax audits conducted with AI assistance in the UK, France, Spain, Italy, and Germany between 2018 and 2022. While the numbers are still modest, there is a noticeable upward trend, especially because AI can analyse large data sets rapidly, making it easier to detect tax fraud.

Nevertheless, the full potential of AI in this area has yet to be realised. Tax authorities are still working on building the necessary skills, including training personnel, a key area of focus for immediate improvement. It is, however, plausible that the percentage of tax audits using AI will continue to grow in the coming years.

Enhancing the quality of service, making better decisions for clients, and identifying new ways to improve services will enable tax professionals to focus on higher-value activities, driving business growth. By identifying new opportunities, improving efficiency, and reducing costs, AI has the potential to increase revenue and profitability for those who know how to use it wisely.

Year	UK	France	Spain	Italy	Germany
2018	10%	8%	5%	6%	9%
2019	15%	12%	8%	9%	14%
2020	22%	18%	13%	14%	20%
2021	30%	25%	20%	21%	28%
2022	40%	35%	30%	30%	38%
2023	52%	48%	42%	40%	50%
2024	65%	60%	55%	52%	63%

Fig 4 Ch, 4 - AI Tool Adoption by Tax Authorities for Audits (2018-2024)
Note: Percentages represent estimated adoption rates of AI tools by tax authorities for audit activities and are for illustrative purposes only.

AI in Medicine

The field of medicine has witnessed remarkable advancements in recent years, significantly improving the quality of care, intervention efficiency, and early diagnosis of certain conditions.

As previously mentioned in the section on the potential use of quantum computers and artificial intelligence, there will be a significant boost in research regarding the improved utilisation of messenger mRNA vaccines.

However, the use of artificial intelligence is already **highly advanced in medical diagnostics,** where it can assist in identifying and diagnosing diseases by analysing vast amounts of medical data and images, particularly in the field of tumour, aneurysm, and other pathology identification. Due to the large volume of information that machine learning models can manage, they can help doctors identify conditions earlier and with greater precision. There are numerous examples of lesion or tumour identification through meticulous analysis of radiological images. It is crucial, however, that the data be accurate, complete, and representative of the population to which the machine learning algorithms will be applied. Furthermore, it is important to utilise data pre-processing techniques and dimensionality reduction methods to eliminate redundant or irrelevant data. To address the challenge of result interpretation, it is essential to develop transparent and comprehensible machine learning algorithms so that doctors and healthcare professionals can understand how AI models have generated their decisions. Moreover, it is crucial to validate AI models accurately and rigorously - see the chapter on ethics and the role of the Digital Ethics Officer.

In the so-called "Life Science" branch, considerable support is provided for **identifying new drugs** and developing personalised therapies. For instance, AI can be used to analyse large amounts of genetic and molecular data to identify new therapeutic targets and personalise cancer treatments. In the field of new drug introduction, it plays a fundamental role in reducing development phase timelines, collecting data by correcting errors, making test result predictive analysis more efficient, and then monitoring behaviour once the drug has been released to the market.

Successes in **robotic surgery** are increasingly frequent, where AI can be used to guide surgical robots and perform complex surgical procedures with precision and safety. In particular, it allows for less invasiveness and the execution of micro-surgery procedures to remove early-stage tumours with high precision.

While respecting privacy rules, AI can be used to **monitor patients and prevent complications** by analysing data from monitoring devices to identify patients at risk of developing complications. To ensure data privacy, it is important to adopt adequate security measures, such as encryption, data anonymisation, and controlled access to the data itself.

There is also a vast area of intervention to provide **virtual healthcare, such as simple online medical advice and guided responses to patients in minor problem cases** or administrative activities. It is obvious that medical research benefits from the ability to analyse large amounts of data to identify hidden correlations and trends, which can help identify new therapies and care approaches.

AI offers many opportunities to improve medicine, but there are also several challenges that must be addressed in the medical context. First and foremost is data quality to generate accurate and reliable models. In the medical context, data can be heterogeneous and incomplete, which can limit the accuracy of machine learning models.

In no other area is data **privacy as relevant:** managing sensitive patient data is a highly critical aspect. The collection, storage, and processing of data must comply with privacy laws, such as GDPR, to protect patient privacy. It must also be said that the interpretation of results can be difficult to interpret and validate.

Integration with medical practice is another non-secondary aspect; it must be integrated into medical practice safely and effectively, which requires adequate training of doctors and healthcare professionals. Moreover, AI systems must be integrated into existing clinical workflows in a way that does not interfere with the daily activities of doctors and healthcare professionals. This aspect is not trivial. Considering clinical protocols and their approval before use, in the case of correct but innovative AI suggestions, there is a risk of losing the effectiveness of its use if the approval of use cannot be integrated with learning that can change the modus operandi.

And how can we manage the ethical responsibility in case of error?. At present, there is still no jurisprudence that clearly delineates the responsibilities between doctors and AI system producers. It is necessary to develop jurisprudence capable of addressing ethical aspects as well, which will be addressed in the last chapter of this publication.

To effectively integrate AI into medical practice, it is important to **involve doctors and healthcare professionals** from the outset in the design and development of AI systems. Furthermore, it is important to provide adequate training to doctors and healthcare professionals on its integration into clinical workflows.

In conclusion, the integration of AI in medicine presents both immense opportunities and significant challenges. As we move forward, it is crucial to strike a balance between technological advancement and ethical considerations, ensuring that AI serves as a tool to enhance medical practice rather than replace human expertise.

Looking ahead, we can anticipate further advancements in AI-driven medical technologies. We may see more personalised treatment plans based on individual genetic profiles, AI-assisted drug discovery becoming the norm, and virtual health assistants playing a larger role in preventative care. However, as these technologies evolve, so too must our regulatory frameworks and ethical guidelines. The future of medicine will likely involve a synergy between human medical professionals and AI systems, with ongoing dialogue and collaboration to ensure that these technologies are developed and implemented in ways that prioritise patient care, privacy, and safety. As we navigate this exciting frontier, continuous education and adaptation will be key for all stakeholders in the healthcare ecosystem.

Human Resources Management

Human resource management is a key factor for an organisation's success, starting from personnel recruitment where AI systems can be used to improve the search and interview process through analysis of candidate data and evaluation of their skills and abilities. For example, **AI can be used to examine candidates' CVs, identify keywords, and evaluate their work experiences** to identify the most suitable candidates for the position. Additionally, AI can be used to create personalised and targeted job advertisements based on demographic and geographic data[13]

Further along in the process, once a candidate has been identified, AI systems can be used to **improve the onboarding process by creating a personalised experience** that supports their individual needs, such as a tailored training plan for each employee based on their knowledge and skills, and provide information on company policies and procedures .

In the daily management of time and attendance, depending on the company's situation, AI has the ability to help manage employee time and attendance efficiently and accurately by evaluating data on employee working hours and predicting future staffing needs [4]. Based on the activity portfolio, it can optimally adjust attendance and unavailability.

Based on the organisation's future projects and strategies, **AI can be used to provide personalised training and development** to employees by analysing data on their skills and training needs, creating a customised training plan for each employee based on their knowledge and competencies. In the long run, this can also influence company culture by promoting collaboration

---

[13] S. Armstrong B. Mitchell *"The Essential HR Handbook"* New Page Books,US 2019

and interaction, and can also be an opportunity to provide more frequent and personalised feedback to employees to help them in their professional growth.

It should be considered that in this field, AI should be used as a support tool but should not completely replace human interaction. At every stage, the final decision on any action should be made by a human manager

For this reason, operators should be involved from the beginning in the design and development of AI systems for human resources, so that they can understand how AI works and how it can be used to improve their work.

The prerequisite is training employees on the use of Artificial Intelligence and its limitations, to highlight how AI can be used and how it can be integrated into human interaction, including ethical and privacy aspects .

The organisation must then have a control system in place to evaluate the effectiveness of AI and its impact on human interaction. In this way, it will be possible to identify any problems or areas for improvement and make the necessary corrections to ensure a balance between automation and human interaction.

Looking ahead, we can anticipate several developments in the integration of AI in human resources management based on **Advanced Predictive Analytics** AI with systems increasingly sophisticated in predicting employee performance, turnover risks, and potential skills gaps within organisation an **Augmented Decision Making,** because HR professionals will rely more on AI-powered insights for strategic decisions, but human judgment must remain crucial for interpreting and applying these insights.

In the area of Personalised Employee Experience, AI will enable highly customised career development paths, learning experiences, and work arrangements tailored to individual employee needs and preferences. It induces that organisations will need to develop **robust frameworks for ensuring ethical** use of AI in HR processes, addressing issues such as bias, privacy, and transparency. The viable future of HR will likely see a symbiotic relationship between AI systems and human professionals, with each complementing the other's strengths.

Interactions with Psychology

We have already mentioned how neuroscience shares many similarities with the development of AI, especially in areas concerning language processing and the neural model underlying machine learning. However, there are also other domains where AI supports psychology.

One such domain is **diagnostic support for mental health disorders**. AI systems can analyse patient data—such as emotional responses during therapy sessions, clinical history, and biological data—to identify which patients might benefit from specific treatments. For instance, AI has shown potential in suicide prevention through the analysis of symptoms and risk factors. In certain cases, social media activity has been monitored to detect warning signs indicating an increased risk of suicide.

Beyond these critical situations, AI systems can also **assist with therapy by providing "chatbots" that offer emotional and psychological support** to patients. These bots are increasingly employed to help individuals manage stress or provide informational assistance. Similarly, AI systems can identify emotions through facial expression analysis and physiological responses, particularly useful for patients with mood disorders or to assess treatment effectiveness.

ML capabilities are progressively applied to personalise treatment plans, adapting to patients' individual symptoms, risk factors, and responses to therapy. These systems are able to evolve treatment plans based on the patient's needs and treatment outcomes.

Today, AI-driven analysis plays a significant role in psychological research. Predictive functions are employed to assess mental health risks or forecast treatment efficacy. We are also witnessing advancements in assistive technologies, such as robots capable of recognising emotions and assisting people with conditions like Alzheimer's disease.

For therapeutic interventions, AI systems, including virtual reality applications, are being trialled for individuals with post-traumatic stress disorder (PTSD). There is little doubt that technological contributions can enhance the quality of life for many individuals. However, it remains essential for psychologists to adhere to ethical codes in their practice. While technology offers great potential, it lacks the ethical awareness that human professionals possess. Psychologists are bound by regulations designed to protect patient privacy and rights.

In summary, the intersection of AI and psychology presents certain risks, especially concerning sensitive data sharing with programmed machines. Patients may not fully understand how their data is used or protected. The ethical framework must safeguard against improper use of AI, ensuring patient privacy and upholding their rights. In fact in 2019, the United States established a national task force to coordinate AI strategies across various sectors, aiming to foster scientific discovery, economic competitiveness, and national security. By 2023, the Organisation for Economic Co-operation and Development reported that AI had become a global competition, indicating AI's undeniable and crucial role.

The relationship between AI and psychology is symbiotic. As cognitive psychologists and neuroscientists gain deeper insights into brain functions, AI development mirrors human neural pathways. Conversely, AI research informs various psychology subfields, introducing new research topics like AI bias and misuse of AI tools.

Several AI schools of thought—connectionist, symbolic, and analogist— borrow ideas from psychological research. Connectionists compare human neural networks to artificial ones, while AI symbolists view mental processes as logical systems. Reinforcement learning in AI was inspired by behavioural psychology, and developmental psychology's findings on spontaneous discovery influence deep learning research.

Many AI research pioneers, such as Frank Rosenblatt and Geoffrey Hinton, have backgrounds in psychology, cognitive science, or neuroscience. Works like "Artificial Psychology: Psychological Modelling and Testing of AI Systems" explore the bidirectional relationship between AI and psychology, focusing on cognitive architectures and artificial emotions.[14]

AI's role in psychology is expanding rapidly, with notable advancements in AI-driven emotional recognition and mental health support systems **research is currently focusing on creating more sophisticated AI models that can adapt dynamically to individual patient needs**, improving both diagnostic accuracy and treatment outcomes. This is particularly promising in areas such as early detection of depression or anxiety through wearable technologies that track physiological signals in real-time.

Looking towards the future, we expect AI to become more integrated into routine psychological care by 2030. AI-powered virtual therapists may complement human practitioners, offering more accessible mental health services, especially in underserved communities. However, with this growth, the ethical concerns surrounding data privacy, consent, and the potential for over-reliance on AI will likely become more pronounced. Governments and regulatory bodies will need to establish robust guidelines to ensure that AI technologies serve as

---

[14] Chong Ho Yu, "Artificial Intelligence, Machine Learning, and Psychology" Oxford Bibliographies, 2023

a force for good in mental healthcare without compromising patient autonomy or confidentiality.

This forward-looking analysis acknowledges both the incredible opportunities and challenges that AI presents within psychology, highlighting the need for ethical vigilance as these technologies evolve.

Artificial Intelligence in Marketing: Current Trends and Future Prospects

In recent years, enterprises have begun adopting solutions with AI support to provide a personalised approach and manage marketing campaigns with the aid of targeted analytics. There is extensive exploitation of data that consumers, who have transitioned from passive users to protagonists, make available more or less consciously.

Data Analysis and Consumer Behaviour: the analysis of data, purchasing behaviours, and consumer preferences significantly influences strategies, making them more targeted and personalised. This optimisation allows companies to **refine their offerings** based on market trends and provide enhanced assistance to both customers and suppliers

Amazon, for instance, utilises AI to personalise product recommendations for customers based on their previous purchases and interactions with the website. Moreover, it employs AI to automate the dispatch of personalised emails and improve the accuracy of product demand forecasts [15].

The personalisation process is, therefore, the first evident effect of AI usage. AI also facilitates automation, such as sending personalised emails, managing social media, and analysing customer data. For instance Netflix employs AI to personalise recommendations for films and TV programmes based on viewing history and preferences, in a loop aimed at increasing the precision of recommendations. Similarly, Spotify uses AI for music recommendations

Consequently, the techniques we've examined in previous chapters, through classifications, can be used to **segment customers into homogeneous groups** based on factors such as age, gender, income, and purchasing preferences. By extension, given the capacity to manage large quantities of data, it's possible to identify market trends, cross-selling opportunities, and areas for product improvement. That's common for retailers like Walmart to

---

[15] T.H. Davenport, R. Ronanki *"Artificial Intelligence for the Real World"* Harvard Business Review, 2018

use AI-powered analytics to segment customers and predict market trends. This allows them to optimise inventory management and personalise marketing efforts.

The **qualitative leap**, however, lies in the **predictive capabilities** regarding customer behaviours, such as purchase probabilities, cart abandonment, and churn rates. As example Telecommunications companies like Vodafone are using AI to predict customer churn and implement proactive retention strategies [16].

Additionally, **the "bots"** (software program that operates on the Internet and performs repetitive tasks) of which we've seen some examples allow efficient interaction with customers, providing real-time support and assistance, thereby enhancing the customer experience and thus strengthening loyalty and satisfaction. Companies like Sephora have implemented AI-powered chatbots to provide 24/7 customer support, product recommendations, and even virtual try-on experiences [17].

Another use of artificial intelligence tools in marketing is in the **creation of visual materials** for marketing campaigns. Apart from ChatGPT, which we've already discussed, there are other similar products that use AI to produce content based on a given topic, paraphrases to find new ways to present company projects, and automatically manage emails, social media, etc. Tools like Jasper.ai and Copy.ai are being used by marketing teams to generate ad copy, social media posts, and even long-form content, significantly speeding up the content creation process.

In summary, many companies have successfully utilised AI in marketing, personalising customer experiences and automating marketing activities. It is clear that the approach may expose the user if ethical and transparent use is not kept under control, ensuring the privacy of customer data and respect for their rights.

In addition to the already mentioned AI Act release in 2024, since years companies operating in the EU should be compliant to GDPR (General Data Protection Regulation) and the correct use of AI may ensure compliance with GDPR itself, automatically managing data consent and providing customers with control over their personal information.

Looking ahead, the integration of AI in marketing is poised to become even more sophisticated and pervasive. AI will enable marketers to **create individualised experiences** for each customer, tailoring not just content but also

---

[16] Ascarza et al."Retention Futility: Targeting High-Risk Customers Might Be Ineffective" Journal of Marketing Research, 2018

[17] Pantano & Pizzi, 2020)."*Artificial intelligence and the new forms of interaction: Who has the control when interacting with a chatbot?*", Journal of Business Research, 2020

product offerings and pricing in real-time. It looks scary for the user because AI models will not only **predict customer behaviours** but also suggest optimal intervention points and **strategies to influence** that behaviour, recognising and responding to human emotions. If in one side it's allowing for more empathetic and effective marketing communications in the other **questions on freedom of choice** of the single user arise immediately.

Through **Augmented and Virtual Reality** marketing with AI will power immersive experiences, allowing customers to interact with products and brands in virtual environments and voice assistants and image recognition technology become more prevalent,

From a positive side we can envision the use of **blockchain** (a digitally distributed, decentralised, public ledger that exists across a network) with AI. That could provide unprecedented levels of transparency and trust in marketing transactions and data management and as well rather than replacing human marketers, all the above, if well organised and structured, will augment their capabilities, handling data analysis and routine tasks while humans focus on strategy and creativity in a useful and respectful for users approach..

As we move towards this AI-driven future in marketing, it will be crucial to **maintain a balance between technological advancement and ethical considerations**, ensuring that the power of AI is harnessed responsibly for the benefit of both businesses and consumers.

The Financial Sector and AI Integration

In 2020, global investments in artificial intelligence (AI) within the financial and insurance sectors were estimated at $50 billion. By 2024, these investments are projected to more than double to over $110 billion, a growth accelerated by the COVID-19 pandemic, which has impacted a variety of financial activities.

AI applications are widespread in asset management and algorithmic trading. However, its influence extends to risk underwriting and blockchain-based services, especially in the case of virtual currencies, where AI is becoming an indispensable tool

AI is used to process large volumes of financial data in real time, allowing **algorithms to make trades** faster than any human could. High-frequency trading (HFT) systems, powered by AI, can predict market trends, identify patterns, and execute trades within microseconds.

AI is also progressively being integrated into blockchain applications, especially for automating **smart contracts.** These contracts execute themselves when specific conditions are met, reducing the need for intermediaries in sectors such as real estate, insurance, and financial services. For instance, the combination of AI and blockchain can streamline claim settlements in insurance by automatically verifying claims and releasing payments once certain conditions are met.

In insurance, AI-powered underwriting systems assess vast datasets to calculate the risk profiles of individuals more accurately than traditional methods (**risk underwriting**). AI models take into account non-traditional data, such as social media activity and internet behaviour, to offer more personalised insurance premiums.

The expansion of AI in financial markets involves policymakers and **regulatory authorities,** given the potential of AI to affect the stability of financial institutions. As we have seen one significant risk is the lack of interpretability and transparency in AI decision-making mechanisms, a challenge often referred to as "explainability". This challenge is particularly pronounced in systems that employ deep learning, where decisions are derived from complex neural networks with multiple hidden layers.

The systemic risks associated with AI include the procyclicality of financial markets. Unintended feedback loops in algorithmic trading can amplify market trends, leading to greater volatility. A lack of transparency in AI's decision-making can also erode trust between institutions and their customers.

Explainability, or the ability to understand unexpected behaviours with clarity and transparency, is critical for making AI applications compliant with current regulations. This is particularly important in the context of neural networks. If not addressed adequately, these systems could become incompatible with existing financial risk management frameworks and supervisory controls.

Looking to the future, continuous evaluation of emerging risks and financial models will be paramount. Financial institutions will need to monitor data quality rigorously to avoid biases in AI-driven decisions. This is especially relevant in underwriting and loan applications, where historical biases could lead to discriminatory outcomes if left unchecked. As such, mechanisms like **kill switches**, which allow for the immediate shutdown of AI systems during exceptional situations, are becoming standard practice, ensuring operational safety much like emergency brakes on trains.

Another key area is "governance structures". Establishing clear governance frameworks will be essential to delineate accountability. This will help prevent uncontrolled networks of neural connections when APIs (Application Programming Interfaces) are exposed to external actors. Without these controls, AI systems could develop behaviours or interactions that elude oversight.

By 2030, AI is expected to induce big changes to the financial sector, driving unprecedented automation such as wealth management, credit assessment, and fraud detection. However, this transformation will necessitate significant investment in internal capabilities within financial institutions and regulatory authorities. In different words enhanced AI literacy will be required to manage and control these systems effectively, balancing innovation with risk.

The future landscape of finance will likely see AI-powered systems making instantaneous decisions on credit applications, portfolio adjustments, and risk management strategies. However, this will only be feasible with robust "ethics frameworks" in place to manage the trade-offs between efficiency, fairness, and transparency.

Decentralised Autonomous Organisations

Blockchain technology has revolutionised the way we think about organisations. By providing a decentralised, transparent, and immutable ledger, blockchain enables the creation of **Decentralised Autonomous Organisations (DAOs)** [18]. While DAOs have gained significant traction in the decentralised finance (**DeFi**) space, their potential extends far beyond financial applications.

Beyond DeFi, DAOs offer a unique governance model that can be applied to a variety of real-world challenges. Two particularly promising areas are commons management and energy management.

- ***Commons Management***: DAOs can facilitate the collective management of **shared resources** like forests, fisheries, or digital assets. Through smart contracts can automate the rules and regulations **governing the use** of these resources, ensuring fairness and transparency, in fact by **tokenising** ownership of the commons, DAOs can create a more inclusive and democratic governance model.
- ***Energy Management***: DAOs can be used to manage and distribute **renewable energy** resources more efficiently, as example smart contracts can automate the trading of energy within local **micro-grids,** empowering communities to **create and manage** their own **energy cooperatives**.

Looking around carefully we could discover that several DAOs are already exploring similar use cases, like the world known Moloch DAO that has been used for funding open-source projects and public goods.

As every new approach DAOs present a unique set of regulatory challenges due to their decentralised nature and the use of blockchain technology. The Jurisdictional Uncertainty because they often operate across multiple jurisdictions, making it difficult to determine which laws apply, especially because

---

[18]M. Field, " *The DAO Handbook: A Guide to Decentralised Autonomous Organisations*", 2021

many countries lack specific regulations for DAOs. They combine elements of corporations, cooperatives, and partnerships, making it **difficult to classify them under existing legal frameworks** creating an hybrid approach and making difficult determining whether members should have limited liability is a complex issue. Same situation in term of **taxation** because they may be considered taxable entities, but **determining their tax residency and the appropriate tax regime can be challenging,** especially for the taxation of tokens issued by DAOs that varies widely across jurisdictions.

If DAO tokens are considered securities, they **may be subject to securities regulations,** including registration and disclosure requirements as well as compliance with Anti-money laundering (AML) and counter-terrorism financing (CTF). Focusing on consumers the decentralised nature of these organisations can be challenging as well as determining **who is responsible for product liability** in the context of a DAO. can be complex.

Data Privacy as well may raise concerns because they may collect and use personal data, especially when DAOS transfer data across borders, which may be subject to data privacy regulations. Ensuring fair and **transparent decision-making processes** , can be difficult, especially when governance is decentralised because the opacity can create the need of dispute resolution, challenging due to the lack of traditional legal structures.

Addressing these regulatory challenges requires a **collaborative approach involving regulators, industry participants, and legal experts**. Developing clear and consistent regulatory frameworks that balance innovation with consumer protection and market integrity is essential for the continued growth and development of DAOs. The potential applications of DAOs are anyway vast and continue to evolve.. As this field matures, we can expect to see even more innovative use cases emerge.

Visual Arts and Multimedia

The introduction of new technologies has always facilitated the creation of new art forms. Photography and cinema are among the most recent examples. Artificial Intelligence (AI) began to influence the visual arts in 2017 when Google launched Deep Dream, one of the first image generators. Although its graphic capabilities were limited, it marked the beginning of AI's role in creative processes.

With the advancements in AI programmes such as DALL-E, Stable Diffusion, and MidJourney, social networks are now filled with peculiar and striking images, immediately recognisable as something novel. These AI systems are "text-to-image" models, and they differ from traditional photography in that the images are generated from text commands ranging from the simplest to the most complex. These models are continuously updated, and the quality of their results is astonishing; in many cases, it is indistinguishable from human-created art. Moreover, the speed is remarkable, with tasks that would have taken human artists days now achievable in just a few hours.

Image generators are increasingly used in **graphic design**, particularly for prototyping and concept art. For example, designers use AI tools to quickly generate multiple design iterations for branding or marketing campaigns, significantly reducing the time spent on early drafts. This technology enables agencies to respond faster to client needs and enhances creativity by generating concepts that may not have been immediately considered by human designers.

While some art critics argue that the artist remains the one who provides the command to the machine, the situation in illustration and graphic professions is more complex. AI-generated images pose a threat to traditional professions, as companies can now create high-quality visuals without hiring human illustrators. This has raised **ethical concerns about whether AI systems infringe on intellectual property rights.** These models are trained on billions of images scraped from the internet, often without the consent of the original artists.

In addition AI-generated content raises concerns about authenticity, especially in the context of deepfakes, where AI is used to create hyper-realistic but false images or videos of individuals. Deepfakes have been used to create misleading media, which could be weaponised for disinformation campaigns or identity fraud. Legally, this enters the realm of image rights, where AI-generated content challenges existing intellectual property laws by using vast databases of existing works to produce new content.

European regulations are introducing the **use of watermarks** to identify whether a graphic work has been created with the assistance of Artificial Intelligence. This is to protect works created manually and their related rights. After all, photography also caused quite a stir when it was first introduced, but it eventually evolved into an art form distinct from painting, which it had been considered a direct competitor and, in a way, a usurper

By 2030, AI is expected to become a mainstream tool in visual arts, with artists, graphic designers, and filmmakers leveraging AI to enhance their creative processes. AI will likely be recognised as a new art form, with "prompt creators" gaining recognition for their ability to guide AI in creating complex and meaningful works. This trend could lead to new industries around AI-assisted art, where the role of human creativity is focused on curating and interpreting AI outputs rather than crafting every detail manually.

Generative AI is rapidly expanding into multimedia fields, from music composition to creating PowerPoint presentations complete with charts and images. AI is moving beyond text and image generation into fields that require a more complex understanding of user inputs. For example, Google's AI can now generate music from a simple text prompt. Based on this model, it is becoming possible to transform a hummed melody into music performed by various instruments. Models like OpenAI's MuseNet and Google's MusicLM as other ones have demonstrated their ability to **generate music in various styles**, from classical symphonies to jazz improvisations. This is particularly useful in industries like film and video game production, where background scores can now be generated by AI, saving both time and resources. Additionally, AI can assist musicians in composing new pieces, offering harmonic suggestions or even generating entire compositions based on a theme.

These system's ability to generate scripts, storylines, and even trailers is transforming the entertainment industry. Scriptwriting AI, for instance, can quickly generate ideas, structure plots, or assist with character development. Companies like ScriptBook have developed AI tools to predict the commercial success of scripts by analysing their narrative and emotional elements.

Artificial Intelligence and **video games** have long been closely intertwined, as games provide fertile ground for machine learning algorithms to improve their capabilities. AI is used to enhance the intelligence and expressiveness of non-playable characters (NPCs), simulate realistic environments, and match players with opponents of similar skill levels. DeepMind, a leading AI company owned by Google's parent company, Alphabet Inc., uses Atari 2600 console games to test its deep learning algorithms. One of its most famous achievements is the creation of AlphaGo, an AI system that defeated the Korean Go champion Lee Sedol in 2016.

AI is now used to generate vast, explorable open-world environments that would be too complex to create manually. For instance, in games like *Assassin's Creed Odyssey*, AI-generated environments allow players to explore a recreated version of Ancient Greece, complete with detailed regions, islands, and cities. AI is also used to create facial expressions and character interactions dynamically, enhancing immersion by allowing NPCs to respond realistically to changing scenarios. At the same time is used to improve player safety and maintain fair play. Microsoft's Project Artemis, for example, applies AI to analyse player interactions and detect inappropriate behaviour, including harassment and cheating. The system helps ensure that online gaming remains a positive experience by identifying disruptive users quickly and efficiently.

Looking ahead, AI will revolutionise the video game industry by enabling more immersive and adaptive gaming experiences. AI-generated environments will become more dynamic, with NPCs that can adapt and learn from player actions in real time. Additionally, AI will play a crucial role in enhancing player safety by continuously monitoring interactions for harmful content. As gaming increasingly incorporates AI-generated content, we can also expect AI to contribute to personalising game experiences based on player preferences and behaviours. The potential for generative **AI across various professional fields is expanding rapidly**. At an experimental level, there are already hundreds of prompts (user interface requests) catering to a wide range of professions. Beyond the capabilities already highlighted, it's crucial for professionals to remain consciously aware of the technology's advancements. Here are some of the most well-known generative AI platforms currently available for different sectors, bearing in mind the daily proliferation of new applications. In the future, AI-generated multimedia will likely become a standard part of production workflows across creative industries. As AI continues to evolve, it will be capable of generating fully interactive multimedia experiences, from dynamic soundtracks that adapt in real time to audience responses to immersive environments in video games that evolve based on player input. We can expect AI to play a central role in the development of augmented reality (AR) and virtual reality (VR) content, creating more personalised and responsive user experiences.

Category	Platform	Description
Text	ChatGPT	Advanced language model for generating text, translating languages, writing different kinds of creative content, and answering your questions
	Bard	Google AI chatbot that can provide summaries of factual topics or create stories.
	Jasper.ai	AI writing assistant designed to help writers create various types of content, from blog posts to marketing copy.
Image	Stable Diffusion	Generates highly detailed images from text descriptions, enabling photo-realistic imagery, art, logos, and more.
	Midjourney	Popular platform for creating images from text descriptions, known for its artistic style and community-driven features.
	DALL-E 2	Generates photo-realistic images and art from a variety of text descriptions.
	Adobe Firefly	Adobe's AI-powered image generation tool, integrated into Adobe Creative Cloud applications.
Video	RunwayML	Platform for creating AI-powered videos, offering features like style transfer, animation, and green screen removal.
	Synthesia	Creates realistic videos of people speaking, using AI to generate the visuals and audio.
	Wonderstudio	AI-powered video editing platform, simplifying complex video production tasks.
Audio	MusicLM	Google AI model capable of generating music from text descriptions.
	Jukebox	Generates music in various genres and styles, based on text descriptions.
	ElevenLabs	Platform for creating hyper-realistic AI voices, enabling text-to-speech and voice cloning.
3D	Point-E	Generates 3D models from text descriptions, enabling rapid prototyping and design.
	DreamFusion	Creates 3D models from text descriptions using diffusion models, offering a high level of detail and realism.
Coding	GitHub Copilot	AI-powered code completion tool from GitHub, helping developers write code faster and more accurately.
	Tabnine	AI-powered code completion tool that provides suggestions as you type.
	Amazon Code-Whisperer	Amazon's AI coding companion, offering code suggestions and completing code based on comments.

Part three: Ethics for AI

Chapter 5: Ethical Aspects of "Good AI"

Intelligent technologies have become pervasive in every aspect of daily life, often hidden and not immediately perceptible, affecting sectors like education, manufacturing, healthcare, and security. Modern search engines profile users, suggesting content to read, effectively creating a personalised "digital landscape". Consequently, debates around the spread of fake news through indistinguishable texts, images, and videos are common, as they circulate among groups with specifically attributed profiles.

AI's power in mass communications is immense, with the capacity to influence public opinion through persuasive means. Search engines, widely used daily, increasingly gather user data, sometimes indirectly, enabling them to guide and influence significant social events.

Generative AI like ChatGPT and Bard, launched by major tech companies, are changing the landscape. As observed, ChatGPT is part of the family of AI models based on machine learning, using neural networks to analyse and comprehend text. Specifically, it belongs to the GPT family, models trained through deep learning but fine-tuned by human corrections. This system has become a serious competitor for Google and other browsers, which have responded with similar solutions, providing pre-processed responses to search queries.

This marks a technological revolution, disrupting current business models. Traditional search engines operate by indexing billions of web pages and ranking them, presenting users with lists of hyperlinks. ChatGPT, however, offers something more enticing: a single response based on specific research and synthesised information. Essentially, ChatGPT doesn't reply with a list of links but with a 'pre-digested' synthesised response.

For users, ChatGPT's answers seem more useful compared to previous methods, as they are clear and complete. The main threat posed by ChatGPT lies in its provision of a singular response, eliminating the need for further exploration of other websites. Consumers increasingly favour quick, easy-to-use services, and this shift reduces traditional search engine ad revenue, with fewer reasons to click on ads. According to Bloomberg, about 81% of search engines' $257.6 billion revenue in 2021 came from advertising.

Historically, presenting a list of links as a response opened the door to significant economic interests and manipulation, often influencing public opinion with fake news.

In the case of ChatGPT, where it does not disclose the sources of its information – in some cases, it's unclear how it generates its answers – one of its biggest risks becomes evident: sometimes its responses are simply wrong or unverifiable. The frequency of ChatGPT errors and their unintentional nature remains uncertain. However, the impact on users without the knowledge or ability to discern incorrect responses is clear. A widely cited estimate on Twitter suggests that between 2% and 5% of responses may be incorrect, though this figure could be higher. This should make users cautious when using Chat-GPT for important decisions. Despite this, it reached one million users in about five days following its launch on November 30, 2022 – much faster than other tech giants. Instagram took two and a half months, and Facebook ten months to reach the same number of users.

Thus, it's reasonable to question how these new forms of AI, accessible to a broad audience, might become potential creators of public opinion. Algorithms undoubtedly play a key role in this dynamic. The Vatican addressed this issue as early as 2020 through the Pontifical Academy for Life with the publication of the "Rome Call for AI Ethics," an international appeal for the ethical development of artificial intelligence. The appeal has been signed by over 100 organisations, including the Vatican, the European Commission, UNESCO, and the International Telecommunication Union. In 2022, this initiative was continued by the RenAIssance Foundation, promoted by the Pontifical Academy for Life, and endorsed by representatives from major tech corporations such as IBM and Microsoft, as well as representatives from the three major monotheistic religions. This effort culminated in 2023 with the release of the "Ethical Guide to the Use of Artificial Intelligence," a document providing concrete guidelines for the ethical development and use of AI, focusing on human dignity, the common good, social justice, and environmental sustainability.

The Vatican's involvement underscores two key concepts: algor-ethics and algocracy. The former, algor-ethics, refers to the necessity of developing AI ethics based on algorithms guided by ethical principles. Since AI has the potential to radically transform society, this transformation should be steered by strategies that benefit humanity, avoiding the kind of unchecked evolution seen with the internet, which resulted in a control-based capitalism dominated by a few powerful entities.[19]

This leads to the concept of algocracy, a plausible future scenario where AI plays a central role in governing and managing social and economic activities. While this is a plausible prospect, it's important to consider the ethical and social implications of such a transition. This model is not inherently negative but only if it is grounded in controllable ethical principles, an approach necessary for addressing the social challenges posed by AI.

---

[19] P. Benanti "Oracoli. Tra algoretica e algocrazia" Luca Sassella, 2018

The presence of multinational representatives at the signing of the 2022 treaty was no coincidence. The rapid adoption of AI in businesses coincides with a shift towards a customer-centric approach by both public and private entities, as well as a rise in social activism.

"Companies are rewarded not just for providing personalised products and services but for upholding customer values and contributing to the welfare of the society in which they operate," said Sudhir Jha, Senior Vice President and Head of Mastercard's Brighterion unit. This highlights the **importance of creating an ethical framework for AI**, especially as the rapid advancement of algorithmic systems makes it increasingly difficult to understand how AI arrives at its conclusions.

It's essential, therefore, to establish an AI ethical framework that sheds light on the risks and benefits of AI tools and sets guidelines for responsible use. The foundation of this is creating a system of moral principles and techniques to address major social issues (we are human) and avoid poorly structured projects that may have undesirable, potentially harmful consequences. Education is crucial for understanding the policies, key considerations, and potential negative impacts of unethical AI and fake data.

Technology is needed to design AI systems capable of automatically detecting fake data and unethical behaviour. Some predict the adoption of trust fabrics, which would provide a system-wide approach to automating privacy assurance, ensuring data confidentiality, and detecting unethical AI use. Many of these concepts are already present in the recently released European AI Act, which we will explore in more detail in upcoming chapters.

Intelligent technologies are now deeply integrated into every aspect of daily life, often hidden and difficult to perceive, influencing sectors such as education, manufacturing, healthcare, and security. Modern search engines profile users, tailoring content recommendations and creating a personalised "digital landscape." As a result, there is growing concern about the circulation of fake news, with texts, images, and even videos becoming indistinguishable from reality and circulating within groups specifically targeted by profiling algorithms.

The power of AI in mass communication is vast, with the ability to shape and influence public opinion through its persuasive force. Search engines, used every day by millions, gather user data, often indirectly, to steer and condition social events. However, this power is not always neutral and could be used to manipulate significant social outcomes.

The Emerging Risks of AI on Social Systems

While the evolution of AI promises many benefits, it introduces significant risks, particularly in its impact on social systems. AI's increasing role in decision-making, content moderation, and public communication has profound consequences, not only for businesses but also for the broader fabric of society.

The ability to personalise content feeds means it can **influence individual perspectives** without users being aware. This has the potential to create echo chambers, reinforcing existing biases and distorting democratic processes. In the wrong hands, AI could be weaponised to polarise societies further by spreading **misinformation or manipulating** political discourse through targeted ads and synthetic media (e.g., deepfakes).

The first consequence is the **erosion of trust in institutions;** the "black-box" nature, where decision-making processes are opaque, poses a risk to societal trust in public institutions, media, and businesses. If AI systems, used for content recommendation, policy decisions, or even law enforcement, produce biased or unverifiable outcomes, public confidence in these systems will erode. Moreover, AI-driven automation in public services may inadvertently deepen social inequalities if left unchecked, by disadvantaging certain demographics who may not be as digitally literate or are underrepresented in AI training data.

The adoption of AI within businesses and industries is set to revolutionise work, leading to automation in many sectors. This presents a risk of unemployment, especially in roles traditionally performed by humans, such as customer service, logistics, or even journalism. AI could **exacerbate economic inequality**, as wealth concentrates around those who own and control AI technologies, while a large portion of the workforce may be displaced or face reduced job prospects.

Transparency is crucial for building trust in AI systems. Users should have access to clear explanations of how AI models generate their conclusions. To address the "black box" problem, regulators and developers must push for Explainable AI (XAI), which can offer insights into decision-making processes. This would enable users to verify outcomes and question any potential bias or error. Furthermore, accountability frameworks should be established, mandating AI providers to disclose the data sources and algorithms used, and take responsibility for errors or misuse.

Governments and international bodies must work together to **create regulatory safeguards** that ensure AI is used responsibly and ethically. The **European AI Act** is a step in the right direction, but global harmonisation of standards is needed to prevent loopholes. Regulations should focus on preventing the use of AI in malicious ways, such as the dissemination of fake news or discriminatory practices in employment or financial services. Additionally, there should be oversight mechanisms to ensure that AI does not perpetuate existing biases or contribute to widening social inequalities.

An effort though is needed to create users basic understanding of the technologies. Digital literacy programs should be expanded to educate the public on how AI functions, its potential biases, and the importance of critical thinking when engaging with AI-generated content. Empowering users with knowledge will help them identify misinformation and protect themselves from manipulation. AI providers should also ensure that users have the tools to question AI's responses and access alternative sources of information.

"Ca va sans dire" that the first step is to embed ethical principles into AI from the design stage. Algorethics, the practice of guiding AI development with ethical principles, should be mandatory for all developers, and that requires education and change of mindset also for the so called "AI expertises", they should be in condition to auto-audit regularly to ensure their job align with ethical standards, especially when deployed in sensitive areas such as healthcare, law enforcement, or education. **The era of nerds and lone coders is over.** A software solution is no longer judged solely on its technical elegance but on its real-world impact. This means rigorously testing its effects over time, monitoring user behaviour, and promptly addressing any issues that may arise. The stereotype of the caffeine-fueled developer, isolated in their 'coding cave', is a relic of the past. **The goal is no longer simply to create a functional product,** but to **solve real-world problems and deliver tangible value to users.** In addition to technical skills, developers must possess soft skills such as effective communication, teamwork, and a deep understanding of user needs Moreover, AI **developers should collaborate with diverse communities** to ensure that their models are representative of all societal groups, reducing the risk of biased outcomes.

With systems, especially the so called "social", capable of collecting vast amounts of personal data, privacy must remain a top priority. **Users should have greater control over their data,** with the ability to opt out of data collection or request the deletion of their personal information. Technologies such as differential privacy and federated learning can be used to minimise data exposure while still allowing systems to learn and improve.

While the technology offers transformative potential across industries and societies, it also brings inherent risks that must be carefully managed. A balanced approach—one that promotes innovation while safeguarding ethical values and protecting social systems—is essential. By fostering transparency, creating robust regulatory frameworks, educating users, and ensuring ethical development, we can harness AI's power responsibly, ensuring that it serves humanity's best interests and upholds the common good.

The first ethical action to **consider is the dissemination of at least a basic understanding of the functioning and limitations of AI systems,** particularly generative AI, even among non-specialist professionals. This publication, in itself, serves as an initiative moving in this direction.

Various organisations—private, public, and international—are now beginning to develop ethical codes for artificial intelligence (platforms of value), issuing formal declarations on the role of AI in the continued advancement of humanity. These ethical guidelines aim to steer AI use in specific domains to ensure alignment with societal benefits.

Historically, the conversation around ethical AI was first raised by Isaac Asimov in his science fiction works, where he introduced the Three Laws of Robotics (do no harm to humans, obey humans, and protect oneself as long as it doesn't conflict with the previous laws). Over time, technocrats, scientists, and policymakers have worked on safeguards to prevent the misuse of AI. Notably, efforts like those from the MIT have been crucial in this development.

A group of cosmologists at MIT, collaborating with AI researchers and developers, formulated the 23 Asilomar AI Principles at the 2017 Pacific Grove Conference. These principles are designed to guide the beneficial development of AI.

An ethical approach to AI encourages a virtuous cycle where technology serves the greater good, creating a symbiotic relationship between innovation and societal well-being. By embedding ethical principles into AI from the ground up, developers and users are compelled to consider the human impact of technological decisions. We have already anticipated the need of development shifts from purely technical goals to human-centric objectives, prioritising fairness, transparency, responsibility, security and and inclusivity .

It requires **long-term thinking,** that has been **missed** not only for AI and IT technologies but on **several other area of science in the last century**, creating the environmental situation the humanity is currently facing. It encourages collaboration between technologists, ethicists, policymakers, and users to co-create solutions that respect societal values. **This multi-disciplinary approach,** that is in AI since the Dartmouth workshop in 1956, ensures that AI development, and overall science and technology that now can't anymore work without, is grounded in a shared vision of public good, where technological advancements support social welfare rather than unchecked corporate gain.

The user becomes centric because is responsible and the focus on education plays a crucial role, as we have seen, promoting digital literacy.

In summary, **ethical AI frameworks** are not just a set of guidelines—they are **a commitment to responsible innovation** that prioritises humanity's well-being. By fostering a culture of ethics, AI can be a force for positive societal transformation, addressing global challenges while safeguarding fundamental human rights and values. **Ethics comes before the rule, as it sets the stage for the rule to be accepted and enacted.**

The UN released principles that are intended to provide a high-level framework for the ethical development and use of AI. Specific implementations may vary depending on the context and application UN Principles for the Development of Artificial Intelligence

Principle	Description
Respect for human dignity	AI systems should be designed and operated to respect the inherent dignity and rights of individuals, in accordance with the Universal Declaration of Human Rights and international human rights law.
Prevention of harm	AI systems should be designed and operated to prevent harm, including physical or psychological harm, to individuals or to society as a whole.
Fairness and non-discrimination	AI systems should be designed and operated to be fair and non-discriminatory.
Transparency	AI systems should be designed and operated in a transparent manner, allowing for understanding and accountability.
Responsibility and accountability	Those who design, develop, and deploy AI systems should be held accountable for their operation and any harmful outcomes.
Privacy	AI systems should be designed and operated with respect for the privacy of individuals.
Security and safety	AI systems should be designed and operated securely, to protect against malicious use and to prevent unintended harm.
Environmental well-being	The development and deployment of AI should be sustainable and respect the environment.
Collaboration	There needs to be international and multistakeholder collaboration on AI governance.

Fig. 1 Ch. 5 -UN Principles for the Development of Artificial Intelligence

The 23 Asilomar Principles

In this light, the 23 Asilomar principles [20] (coordinated by Future of Life Institute and developed at the Beneficial AI 2017 conference), are one of the earliest and most influential sets of AI governance principles and can be viewed as a first opening for the development of a common ethics and applied in various ways depending on specific research contexts. Below is a summary of how they relate to AI, the complete list is available in Appendix.

Asilomar Principles	Research Problems	Ethics and Values	Long-Term Problems
Transparency	Lack of transparency in AI	Right to knowledge and	Abuse of AI systems for harmful or
Accountability	Possibility of harm or prejudice caused by AI systems	Right to safety and protection	Loss of human control over AI systems
Non-maleficence	Possibility of physical or psychological harm caused by AI systems	Right to health and well-being	Unemployment and marginalization caused by AI
Benefit to humanity	Possibility of harmful or unjust uses of AI systems	Right to progress and well-being	Unequal distribution of AI benefits
Independence	Possibility of manipulation or control of AI systems by private interests	Right to freedom and self-determination	Loss of national sovereignty caused by AI
Respect for life	Possibility of using AI systems for purposes that violate human dignity	Right to life and dignity	Creation of sentient or conscious AI systems

Fig. 2 Ch. 5: Summary of the Asilomar Principles

It is important to note that these principles are continuously evolving. Their core focus remains on research challenges, ethics, values, and long-term issues. Given that AI is now common in almost every branch of science, it is inevitable that these principles be shared universally. This leads to the conclusion that all research, irrespective of its subject, is no longer immune to ethical risks, even in technological fields that may initially seem distant from such concerns.

Transparency and Responsibility have now become essential across the entire technological landscape. The introduction of the internet provides a clear example: once hailed as a tool for democratising information, it has become the foundation of what is now referred to as "surveillance capitalism" [21],

---

[20] FLI, The Asilomar AI Principles https://futureoflife.org/open-letter/ai-principles/, 2017

[21] S. Zuboff *"The Age of Surveillance Capitalism"* William Collins 2021

where user data is classified based on opaque criteria, often excluding the most vulnerable members of society. This, in essence, contradicts the internet's original promise. The principles of non-maleficence and benefit to humanity should now be integral to all forms of research, particularly when part of the work is carried out autonomously by machine-learning systems or includes generative AI.

In all forms of research, the potential social impacts of systems must be considered in advance to prevent their harmful or unjust use. The most challenging aspect concerns anticipating long-term problems. Autonomy, respect for life, and non-maleficence should guide AI's independence from private interests that could cause physical or psychological harm to the most vulnerable.

The Asilomar principles provide a valuable framework for guiding the development of science and AI responsibly and sustainably. These principles have served as a reference for regulations that have been issued or are in progress in various regions around the world.

The Asilomar principles offer a valuable starting point, but as AI technologies rapidly evolve, these guidelines must adapt to the new challenges and opportunities that arise. Around the world, governments, corporations, and civil societies are recognising the need for ethical governance frameworks that ensure AI serves humanity's best interests. The global evolution of these principles reflects a broader understanding that AI can transform society positively if developed with responsibility, transparency, and a commitment to the common good. As these principles continue to evolve, they will shape a future where AI is a force for societal progress, equity, and human dignity.

Let's now revisit the aspects related to regulations in various geographies to analyse them in light of what we've examined thus far.

The group of European regulations, including the "AI Act", "Digital Market Act" (DMA), and "Digital Service Act" (DSA), and "Data Act" follow a risk-based approach and establish obligations for providers and users depending on the level of risk the system may generate. Some systems with an unacceptable level of risk to people's safety are severely prohibited, including systems that use subliminal or manipulative techniques, exploit people's vulnerabilities, or are even used for "social scoring" (classifying people based on their social behaviour, socioeconomic status, and personal characteristics).

In this direction, Google, Microsoft, Anthropic, and OpenAI, four leading companies in the race for next-generation artificial intelligence, announced in July 2023 the creation of a new professional organisation to counter associated risks.

The new organisation, called "Partnership on AI" (PAI), aims to promote the safe and responsible development of AI and mitigate potential risks associated with this technology. PAI is also committed to ensuring that AI is used for the benefit of humanity and does not cause harm.

The creation of PAI has represented an important step towards greater transparency and accountability and is also a signal that industry leaders are determined to ensure that AI is used safely and responsibly. However, it is still an organisation of leading companies in the IT world that aim to advance research and aim, in order to exist, at profitability. In the United States, there is also the "Frontier Model Forum", whose members commit to sharing best practices with legislators, researchers, and associations to make these new systems less dangerous.

Unlike Europe, where the main role is now in the hands of public entities, in the United States, political tensions in Congress have prevented any efforts in this direction. The White House has therefore encouraged relevant groups to ensure the safety of their own products on their own, in the name of their "moral duty", by adhering to "three principles" in AI development (cybersecurity, personal safety, and trust). The decision to ask industry companies for a formal commitment without imposing laws and regulations has been described by US newspapers as a way to obtain greater collaboration from private entities with institutions and not to hinder a rapidly developing sector. The path that is taking shape is that of thorough software testing before making it public, including through the opinion of independent experts. However, this approach may not reassure everyone, considered riskier, for example, than the European one, based on ethical "guardrails" imposed by institutions.

It is nevertheless positive to see that there is growing attention to AI safety and responsibility and that major industry players are already working to address potential associated risks.

China has also moved, publishing new rules but with exclusive reference to generative AI, that is, the subset of AI to which ChatGPT belongs, with the ability to converse in a "human" way and generate "new" texts or images. The Chinese measures aim not only to promote innovative and high-quality use of generative AI but also to protect the intellectual property rights involved. On 13 July 2023, the Cyberspace Administration of China - the country's main Internet control and censorship system - published a series of guidelines to regulate the generative AI sector, the so-called "Interim Measures for the Management of Generative Artificial Intelligence Services", which came into effect in mid-August 2023. In this way, the People's Republic of China intends to "promote the innovative use of generative AI in various sectors and fields, which generates positive, healthy, and encouraging high-quality content", as well as support enterprises, educational and research institutions, public and professional cultural institutions that contribute to technological innovation of generative AI. However, it remains evident that generative AI service providers are obliged to "conduct security reviews and register their algorithms with the government in accordance with the 'Regulation on the Management of Recommendations on Algorithms for Internet Information Services', if their services are capable of influencing public opinion or 'mobilising' the public"; this is a clear confirmation of how the Chinese legislator proposes, on one hand, to regulate the effects of recommendation algorithms on the life and web experience of Chinese users, on the other hand, to impose greater transparency on operators, as well as a "fair" use of algorithms "aimed at good".If we want to make a broad comparison with Brussels' "AI Act", one of the main differences between the two regulations is that Beijing's regulation remains strictly limited to generative AI, while the EU's AI Act, in its current version, extends to AI in its entirety.

The new draft of Chinese regulation has also defined an "ad hoc" protection for intellectual property rights involved in generative AI training processes, expressly establishing that providers and users of generative AI services will have to "respect intellectual property rights and business ethics, protect trade secrets and not practice monopoly or unfair competition by exploiting algorithms, data, platforms, and other advantages".

This is different from the provisions of the "AI Act", which provides for an obligation of prior authorisation for AI service providers, who are required to list in advance "any copyrighted content included among the data used for training".

The Chinese legislator has gone further, also providing that service providers, in carrying out AI training data selection activities (such as preliminary training and optimisation training), in case intellectual property rights are involved, to be compliant with the law "should not in any way violate those rights and related interests of others".

The Chinese perspective focuses on copyright protection for works created through the use of generative AI and differs from the anthropocentric approach adopted by the European Union.

The following table summarises the main characteristics of AI regulations in various geographic areas.

We are interested in the salient points, as already anticipated in the introduction, that the three geographic areas adopt different approaches, which reflect different values and objectives.

These are, however, regulations in continuous development but which already denote clear trends on the focus of various geographic and political areas, which must be taken into account, considering that the evolution of technology will certainly contemplate changes.

Characteristic	USA	Europe	China
Regulatory Approach	Primarily market-based, focusing on voluntary guidelines and industry self-regulation.	A mix of market-based and regulatory approaches, with a strong emphasis on data protection and privacy.	A combination of market-based and regulatory approaches, with a focus on national security and economic development.
Key Regulatory Bodies	Federal Trade Commission (FTC), Equal Employment Opportunity Commission (EEOC), Department of Transportation (DOT)	European Union General Data Protection Regulation (GDPR), European Commission, national data protection authorities	Cyberspace Administration of China (CAC), Ministry of Science and Technology (MOST)
Data Privacy	Strong focus on data privacy, particularly for personal data.	Very strict data privacy regulations, including the GDPR.	Relatively strict data privacy regulations, with a focus on national security and economic development.
Algorithmic Fairness	Increasing focus on algorithmic fairness and bias mitigation.	Growing emphasis on algorithmic fairness and transparency.	Developing regulations to address algorithmic bias and discrimination.
Autonomous Systems	Developing regulations to address the safety and ethical implications of autonomous systems.	Developing regulations to address the safety and ethical implications of autonomous systems, with a focus on road vehicles.	Developing regulations to address the safety and ethical implications of autonomous systems, with a focus on national security and economic development.
International Cooperation	Increasing international cooperation on AI regulation, including through the Global Partnership on AI.	Active participation in international AI governance initiatives.	Increasing international cooperation on AI regulation, with a focus on promoting Chinese AI technology and standards.

Fig 3 Ch 5 Comparison of AI Regulations in the USA, Europe, and China

Transparency and Fairness in the EU Proposal

Let's take a look into how European legislation seeks to address the points we've discussed thus far.

Figure 2 Chapter 5 attempts to exemplify the innovative approach that does not impose regulatory limits on any technology itself, but rather places controls, up to prohibition, on the type of use if it conflicts with the principles of fairness, transparency, and responsibility analysed thus far.

It's a modern legislative approach because, by focusing on the citizen, it doesn't limit technological development but merely defines prohibited or high-risk areas.

AI systems that present an unacceptable risk are those that can cause physical harm or damage to people's health, or violate their fundamental rights, such as privacy or non-discrimination. Unacceptable risks also include all actions that can cause economic or financial harm. For Title II Chapter 5, these are essentially all risks that may represent exploitation of individual vulnerabilities with both material and psychological damages. "Social scoring" by public or private entities that could lead to discrimination in access to services or work or study activities, up to repressive actions based on statistical evaluations, is banned. Along these lines, real-time biometric identifications in public areas are prohibited, except for serious public order situations that pose risks to the population.

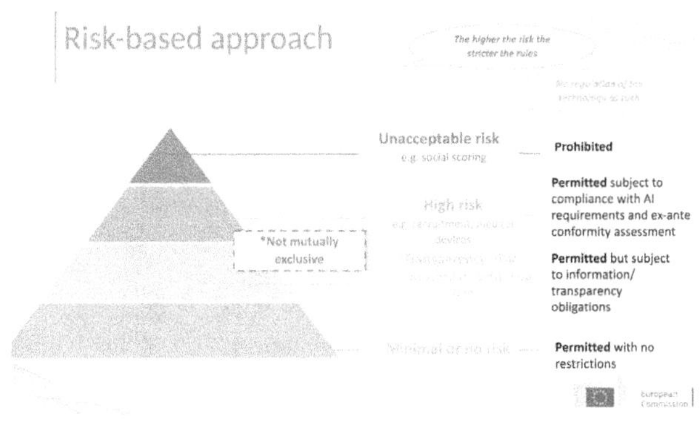

Fig. 4 Ch. 5 - Basic structure of the European AI Act

High-risk systems are those that can cause physical harm or damage to people's health if not used correctly. For example, a system used to diagnose diseases could misdiagnose an illness if not used correctly and effectively violate people's fundamental rights if not used responsibly. This also applies to systems that operate in economic or financial spheres, which, if not used appropriately, could make wrong decisions in relation to inappropriate investments.

A country's strategic structures are also involved, for example, energy production and distribution systems, which represent the basis for supporting, for instance, medical equipment, systems that use biometric data (facial recognition, fingerprints, etc.) to identify and possibly categorise people (number of patients with a certain disease, specific ongoing treatments, etc.).

Already available systems that operate on critical infrastructures are also high-risk. In this case, the difference between autonomy, typical of AI, and automation should be emphasised. Until now, many critical infrastructures such as energy transmission or telecommunications have exploited high levels of automation, which in reality have always shown a certain rigidity and still require continuous monitoring by highly specialised personnel. With the introduction of learning systems and generative capabilities, we move into a terrain of decision-making autonomy of the system, even if only partial, where some operational decisions are intrinsic to the way the learning system operates. An unforeseen operation could have catastrophic effects in the case of an electrical power network of a region and telephone transmissions of entire areas.

For this reason, systems classified as high-risk all require ex-ante, intra-design, and ex-post evaluations, with monitoring over time.

All these activities require the implementation of a "management system" and maximum transparency on the purposes for which they are activated, with control of the data used for training, validation, and testing of the AI system, the definition of appropriate documentation, and possibly limitations on access to information accompanied by an appropriate level of transparency. The system must include the possibility of supervision at any time, and robustness and cybersecurity must be proven.

Some attention in the design and control phase is also required for what are considered controllable risks, which can cause physical harm or damage to people's health, but only in exceptional circumstances, for example in the chaos of lack of maintenance of a co-bot or financial systems not used correctly.

The European regulation for AI provides that AI solutions that present a high or unacceptable risk are subjected to an evaluation and certification process before being placed on the market or put into service in the European Union, in order to minimise associated risks.

The evaluation and certification process should include various phases: the first action is risk assessment: this phase should identify and evaluate the risks associated with the system, which should be followed by measures to mitigate identified risks. The consequence is a certification process that should attest that a given system meets the safety, robustness, and respect for fundamental rights and economic interests of the European Union requirements.

We report this approach because it represents a fundamental step in regulation. Instead of prescribing the "how" and "what", it defines "what to protect", the human being in their role as a citizen with rights and dignity.

In this way, all aspects that we have already analysed previously are guaranteed:

Transparency: The proposed regulation requires AI systems to be transparent and understandable. Information must be provided in a clear and comprehensible manner to the concerned citizens. Therefore, it means that the decision-making processes of algorithms must be understandable and traceable. Explanations should be provided in such a way that people can understand how and why a decision was made. AI system operators must be able to provide information on their operation, the reasons for a particular decision, and the data used.

Fairness: The regulation emphasises the importance of avoiding discrimination and ensuring that solutions do not lead to unfair or discriminatory results. For bias and diversity, it is required to address and mitigate biases in technologies to ensure that there are no unjustified disparities based on characteristics such as gender, age, ethnicity, etc., and above all, it is important that the data used to train the models are representative of the diversity of the populations involved.

Responsibility: Regarding direct responsibility (Accountability), AI system operators are required to assume responsibility for their impact, i.e., they must be able to demonstrate that they have done everything possible to avoid harm or violations, through a demonstrably safe ex-ante design and ex-post Surveillance with Monitoring to continuously monitor and evaluate the operation of systems to identify and correct any issues.

Safety: The protection of data used in systems to ensure the privacy and security of sensitive information and prevent abuse and use for illegal or harmful purposes. Last but not least, compliance with regulations, including local and international laws and regulations relating to data security and privacy.

To these themes, fundamental to ensuring that artificial intelligence is developed and used responsibly and safely, are added the concepts of quality for artificial intelligence, similar to those used for other products and services, albeit with some important differences to consider.

In terms of artificial intelligence, quality can be defined as the extent to which an AI system meets its design objectives and satisfies the needs of its users. Therefore, Effectiveness is the measure of how well a solution achieves its design objectives. And it is an important aspect of quality, as systems must perform the tasks for which they were designed, and it goes along with Efficiency, which is the measure of how efficiently resources are consumed. At this time, it is an important aspect of AI quality, as AI systems need to be able to function economically. **CO2 production remains one of the critical aspects of the use of generative AI** due to high energy demand.

To complete the qualitative characteristics, one must consider Accuracy, which measures how accurately a neural network provides results, along with Completeness, which classifies how well it is able to provide all the necessary information to make informed decisions. Another aspect is that of Flexibility to allow a system to adapt to new needs, working in constantly evolving environments. For this reason, Usability is also necessary to allow a wide range of users. Safety is the measure to evaluate how well an AI solution is protected from attacks or abuse, measuring how well systems are able to protect sensitive data and information.

An aspect highlighted in recent times that can be ascribed to ethical issues is that of energy impact, especially with reference to carbon dioxide production, **the so-called "carbon footprint".**

There have been advances in reducing carbon dioxide released into the atmosphere, such as Meta's "Green AI" initiative. All major IT companies more or less have a plan for energy coverage with renewable energy up to 100%. Neural network training at this moment is in its infancy and cannot even be compared to the operational efficiency of the human brain (just to clarify, the equivalent energy consumption of a human brain has been estimated at around 20 watts).

There are studies that report measurements and optimisation plans for the environmental impact of AI models. The orders of magnitude speak of hundreds of tons of CO2 emitted per day.[22]

Research in this field has had to create measurement tools and new optimisations to reduce the footprint of AI models. There is an "ethical" competition between models that reduce carbon dioxide production which compares various generative AI platforms.

A solution lies in reducing the overall training time, thus reducing the energy needed for training and executing models

These are important advances, but the work is far from finished. The hope is that these measurement and optimisation tools will spread rapidly through the common development of applications as a deontological approach of those working in the sector for responsible AI construction in the long term.

---

[22] International Energy Agency "Electricity 2024 Analysis and forecast to 2026", 2024

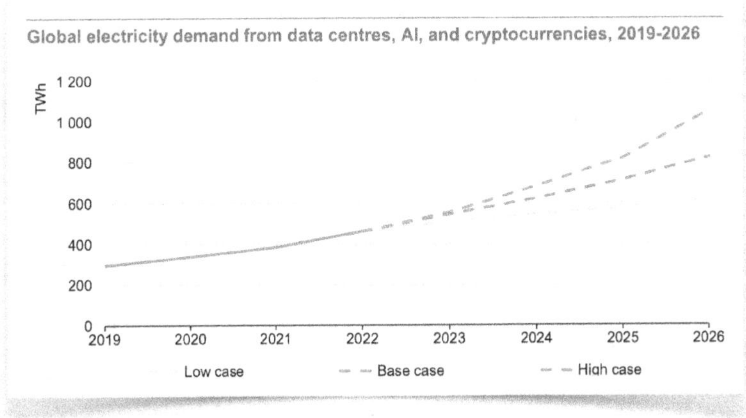

Fig. 5 Ch. 5 Energy consumption related to Data Centres for AI and Criptocurrencies

A mention of improper use, based on what we've already seen, should not be forgotten that the use of AI can originate malicious actions. There have been rumours of research into new chemical weapons designed using AI, it might not be true, but the worrying part is that it is technically possible, as are a myriad of other improper uses.

Artificial intelligence, and particularly ChatGPT, make things easier for potential criminal actions. And "computer forensics" experts are beginning to see cases of artificial intelligence being used illegally. There are already situations of "software stealer" codes (capable of stealing information from victims' computers), based on learning networks and able to search, copy, and extract common file types, such as Office documents, PDFs, and images from systems, if appropriately "infected".

The first line of defence is in the ethics of developers themselves, as they are among the best to assess how their work can be misused. The definition and respect of professional ethics is now an obligation, as in many other older professions.

However, the misuse of technology remains a problem that States, international communities, and intergovernmental processes are addressing, albeit with some slowness and difficulty.

The **EU's AI Act is still in the process** of being finalised and implemented. As AI technology rapidly evolves, regulators face the challenge of keeping pace with new developments while ensuring the legislation remains relevant and effective. And while the EU is taking a leading role in AI regulation, there's a **growing need for global harmonisation** of AI governance to prevent regulatory fragmentation and ensure consistent standards across borders.

The ongoing debate is about finding the right balance between fostering innovation in AI and implementing necessary safeguards. Overly restrictive regulations could potentially slow down innovation and put EU companies at a competitive disadvantage.The emphasis on ethical development though has intensified, with more companies and organisations adopting some form of AI ethics guidelines. However, translating these principles into **practical, enforceable standards remains a challenge.**

As **AI systems become more complex**, ensuring transparency and explainability, especially for high-risk applications, is increasingly challenging but crucial for building trust and accountability and the **growing awareness of AI's carbon footprint** has led to increased research and development in energy-efficient AI models and green computing. With the rapid advancement of AI capabilities, **ensuring the safety and security** of systems, particularly against potential misuse or malicious applications, has become a critical concern for policymakers and developers alike.

Despite increased attention, **addressing bias in AI systems** and ensuring fairness across diverse populations remains a complex and ongoing challenge, requiring continuous monitoring and refinement of AI models and training data. The potential impact on the **job market and workforce skills** is an evolving challenge, requiring adaptive policies and education systems to prepare for AI-driven changes in various sectors. As technology becomes more pervasive in daily life, **there's a growing need to enhance public understanding of AI capabilities** and limitations to build trust and informed engagement with AI technologies.

The Role of the Digital Ethics Officer

There remains the problem for organisations developing innovation through digital projects that include the use of AI to equip themselves with ethics adequate to human values and the challenges of the millennium during the operational concept definition phase.

We have seen that ethical discipline in this field is not yet formalised from a legislative point of view and is not even frequent as a company policy within private or public organisations; sometimes as a deliberate choice, sometimes induced by a focus on objectives without considering the side effects of a specific application.

In the discussions that have recently animated the introduction of AI in many areas, the idea of an organisational role that has the precise responsibility of ensuring respect for ethical aspects for digital projects is beginning to take hold.

This is the **Digital Ethics Officer** (DEO).

The name is not relevant, but a new role is certainly **necessary that must work transversally and with a systemic vision of digital projects**, taking into account the specificities of the activity sector, the territory on which the project will act, and the relevant applicable ethical recommendations.

A sort of conductor of an ethical, legal, and technical system at the service of a digital manager, and must organise, coordinate, and animate reflections on the margins of a digital project of a company or public entity, knowing the roles and responsibilities of the various components of the development team.

Fundamental will be the ability to **connect the different organisational areas**, often organised in silos: administration, research and development, legal, production, communication, marketing, quality, customer service. Each must have its own field of intervention and the DEO must maintain a **clear vision of the process**, facilitating everyone's participation in defining an ethical framework for the organisation's activities.

It is important that this professional manages to maintain a common agreement between the various elements about the values to defend and the ethical rules to put into practice. Therefore must impose an overall vision among the various components. Both in the design phase, design ethics, and in the execution phase, caring about evolution ethics, which ensures consistency over time. The latter is a continuously evolving part and is based on the ability to consider and capitalise on the evolution of ethical, legal, and technical aspects, anticipating the risks associated with a project that exploits AI.

AI encompasses a vast and **complex field of science and technology, ranging from robotics to ChatGPT**. Its overarching goal is to develop computational systems capable of solving problems and performing tasks that would otherwise require human intelligence. The remarkable aspect of AI is that it doesn't necessitate intelligence itself, in the sense that **doesn't have consciousness of what is doing**, image text or code ; it succeeds by operating at 'zero intelligence'. This is made **possible by a confluence of factors**, including massive datasets, increasingly sophisticated statistical and algorithmic tools, and the ongoing digitalisation of the world. We must leverage this new form of capability to act with 'zero intelligence' as a reservoir of opportunities, but with caution and responsibility. While **recognising its immense potential benefits,** we must also acknowledge **the potential risks and catastrophic consequences that could arise from poorly designed or managed AI systems**

The **persuasive power of AI systems**, particularly when coupled with online 'social' biases, is not a primary subject of this book, but it is a topic of intense contemporary debate **and it should be considered by a DEO working in the IT environment to influence the appropriate strategy.**

The significant influence of AI on beliefs and behaviours through personalised, data-driven strategies. By processing vast amounts of data and tailoring content to individual susceptibilities, AI enhances the capabilities of persuasive technology (PT). There are **ethical implications of AI's "hypersuasion"** [23] and its potential to both empower persuaders and disempower the persuadable. The risks of AI's persuasive power being misused by malicious actors are addressed, along with specific strategies to mitigate negative consequences: protecting privacy, fostering competition among persuaders, ensuring accountability through regulation and human values alignment, and promoting digital literacy and public engagement. The goal is to harness AI's power to support better decisions and behaviours while safeguarding individual autonomy and fostering a sustainable society. A lot of academic work around this topic.

We have also seen that **quantum computing and AI continue to converge**, there's a **growing need for specialised ethical frameworks** that address the unique challenges posed by this intersection. The development of "quantum-ELSPI" is a step in the right direction, but it's still in its infancy and requires further development and widespread adoption. The complexity of issues arising from quantum computing and AI **necessitates increased collaboration between scientists, ethicists, policymakers, and industry leaders.** Facilitating effective communication and understanding between these diverse groups remains a significant challenge.

---

[23] L. Floridi *"Hypersuasion-* persuasive power and how to deal with it" Centre for Digital Ethics *2024*

The potential for quantum AI technologies to be **used for both beneficial and harmful purposes (e.g., in cryptography and cybersecurity)** presents significant ethical and security challenges that need to be carefully addressed.

The world is getting more and more complicated while the concept of a **Digital Ethics Officer** is gaining traction, there are challenges in **defining the exact scope of this role**, ensuring its independence within organisational structures, and providing appropriate training and resources for these professionals.

Incorporating ethical considerations into the training of AI (and quantum computing) **professionals** is crucial but challenging, requiring updates to educational curricula and professional development programmes.

Digital Ethics Officer responsibilities

Fig. 6 Ch. 5 DEO responsibility scenario

The **Data Ethics Officer (DEO) needs to be someone, or a team, who people trust and respect,** both inside and outside the company. For smaller businesses, it's easy to think that the DEO should just be a young person who knows a lot about AI. But really, the **DEO should be someone who understands how the company works** and can see the bigger picture of using AI. They need to be experienced and respected, and they need to be able to explain the value of AI to everyone in the company.

For major companies instead is not possible to provide a detailed summary of the exact organisational structures and responsibilities of Digital Ethics Officers (DEOs) across all. Especially large corporations, have diverse organisational structures. The role and placement of a DEO can vary significantly depending on the company's size, industry, internal culture, and regulatory environment. We may say that the role of DEOs is relatively new and still evolving and as technology and ethical considerations continue to change, companies are adapting their organisational structures and DEO responsibilities accordingly.

However, we can sketch a general overview of the common themes and trends observed in DEO roles in Fig. 6 Ch.5.

Common Themes	Typical Responsibilities
Reporting Structure	Directly to CEO, C-Suite, or Board of Directors
Scope of Responsibility	Company-wide ethics policies, AI governance, data privacy, and responsible AI development
Collaboration	Working closely with legal, compliance, HR, and IT departments
Stakeholder Engagement	Interacting with customers, employees, investors, and regulators
Education and Training	Promoting ethical awareness and providing training to employees

Fig. 7 Ch. 5 Common themes for DEO roles

While specific details may not be publicly available, companies like Google, Microsoft, IBM, Amazon, and Facebook have established prominent DEO roles to oversee ethical AI practices. These DEOs often work closely with research teams, product managers, and legal departments to ensure AI is developed and deployed responsibly.

The potential for digital technologies to generate new revenue streams is substantial. However, the proliferation of these technologies, coupled with their unique ethical challenges, has increased the expectation for organisations to consider ethical obligations, social responsibilities, and organisational values when pursuing digital opportunities.

Additionally, there is a growing demand for digital services that are fair, equitable, inclusive, and beneficial to society.

Digital adopters seek technologies that are safe, error-free, and free from harm or abuse. By pursuing digitally responsible growth strategies, organisations can build stakeholder trust and achieve positive outcomes.

This is a challenge, not just for IT and cloud companies, but especially for developers creating professional solutions. They need to think about the ethical side of things, and users should also ask themselves how AI might affect their work, including the impact of those really common social systems that shape our daily lives.

Conclusion

Artificial intelligence is now woven into the fabric of our daily lives. From searching the internet to applying for a loan, finding a job, or even meeting someone new on a dating app, our interactions are shaped by various AI algorithms. Because these technologies operate so seamlessly in the background, their true nature often goes unnoticed.

This publication aims to shed light on these ubiquitous tools, making them more visible and understandable. While it doesn't claim to be exhaustive, it offers a basic introduction to AI for those who are, or will soon be, working with AI-driven solutions.

The goal is to foster awareness and understanding, enabling individuals to make informed decisions and ensure that humans remain at the heart of the decision-making process. This is just the beginning of a long journey that could lead to a better future for all.

While there are risks involved, they primarily lie outside the technology itself and relate to broader societal issues. This is a complex challenge that requires a holistic approach, extending beyond the technical aspects of AI and into the realm of human values and ethics. While this is an ambitious, even utopian goal, it is one that deserves .... another book.

Acknowledgements

Beyond the reader who has perhaps patiently reached this point, I must express my gratitude to the university students I have had the opportunity to meet in Italy and Ireland, and to the members of professional orders, specialists in various disciplines, who have presented me with the diverse perspectives from which people try to understand the utility of Artificial Intelligence.

In particular, I would like to thank the students of the University of Padua, who were very active during the Gregorianum Summer School of 2022 and 2024, and the members of the Order of Engineers of Lecco and Brescia, Italy and the Orders of Journalists of Milan, Bologna and Venice, still in Italy and the ORSi Consilium team in Dublin, an invaluable partner in this project.

Appendix 1

Glossary of AI Acronyms

Acronym	Term	Definition
AI	Artificial Intelligence	The simulation of human intelligence processes by machines, especially computer systems.
ML	Machine Learning	A subset of AI that allows computers to learn from data and improve their performance on a
DL	Deep Learning	A type of machine learning that uses artificial neural networks with multiple layers to learn
NLP	Natural Language Processing	The ability of computers to understand, interpret, and generate human language.
GAN	Generative Adversarial Network	A type of deep learning architecture that pits two neural networks against each other to generate
RNN	Recurrent Neural Network	A type of neural network that processes sequential data, making it suitable for tasks like language
CNN	Convolutional Neural Network	A type of neural network that is particularly effective for processing image and video data.
IoT	Internet of Things	A network of interconnected devices that can collect and exchange data.
RPA	Robotic Process Automation	The use of software to automate repetitive tasks.
AIaaS	AI as a Service	A cloud-based delivery model for AI tools and services.
AGI	Artificial General Intelligence	A hypothetical form of AI that can perform any intellectual task that a human being can.
ASI	Artificial Superintelligence	A hypothetical form of AI that surpasses human intelligence in all aspects.

Appendix 2

AI terminology

Acronym	Term
Bias	A systematic error in a machine learning model that leads to unfair or discriminatory outcomes.
Overfitting	A situation where a model performs well on the training data but poorly on new, unseen data.
Underfitting	A situation where a model is too simple to capture the underlying patterns in the data.
Reinforcement Learning	A type of machine learning where an agent learns by interacting with an environment and receivingrewards or penalties for its actions.
Unsupervised Learning	A type of machine learning where the algorithm learns without labeled data.
Supervised Learning	A type of machine learning where the algorithm learns from labeled data.
Neural Network	A computational model inspired by the structure and function of the human brain.
Neuron	A basic unit of a neural network, similar to a biological neuron.
Activation Function	A function that introduces nonlinearity into a neural network.
Backpropagation	An algorithm used to train neural networks by adjusting the weights of the connections between neurons.
Hyperparameter	A parameter that is set before training a machine learning model, such as the learning rate or number of hidden layers.
Data Mining	The process of discovering patterns and trends in large datasets
Data Science	The interdisciplinary field of extracting insights from data.
Big Data	Extremely large datasets that are difficult to process using traditional data processing tools.
Cloud Computing	The delivery of computing services over the internet.
Edge Computing	Processing data closer to the source, rather than in a centralized data center.

Appendix 3

The 23 Asilomar principles list[24]

Artificial intelligence has already provided beneficial tools that are used every day by people around the world. Its continued development, guided by the following principles, will offer amazing opportunities to help and empower people in the decades and centuries ahead.

Research Issues

1) Research Goal: The goal of AI research should be to create not undirected intelligence, but beneficial intelligence.

2) Research Funding: Investments in AI should be accompanied by funding for research on ensuring its beneficial use, including thorny questions in computer science, economics, law, ethics, and social studies, such as:

- How can we make future AI systems highly robust, so that they do what we want without malfunctioning or getting hacked?
- How can we grow our prosperity through automation while maintaining people's resources and purpose?
- How can we update our legal systems to be more fair and efficient, to keep pace with AI, and to manage the risks associated with AI?
- What set of values should AI be aligned with, and what legal and ethical status should It have?

3) Science-Policy Link: There should be constructive and healthy exchange between AI researchers and policy-makers.

4) Research Culture: A culture of cooperation, trust, and transparency should be fostered among researchers and developers of AI.

5) Race Avoidance: Teams developing AI systems should actively cooperate to avoid corner-cutting on safety standards.

---

[24] Future of Life Institute, https://futureoflife.org/open-letter/ai-principles/

Ethics and Values

6) Safety: AI systems should be safe and secure throughout their operational lifetime, and verifiably so where applicable and feasible.

7) Failure Transparency: If an AI system causes harm, it should be possible to ascertain why.

8) Judicial Transparency: Any involvement by an autonomous system in judicial decision-making should provide a satisfactory explanation auditable by a competent human authority.

9) Responsibility: Designers and builders of advanced AI systems are stake-holders in the moral implications of their use, misuse, and actions, with a re-sponsibility and opportunity to shape those implications.

10) Value Alignment: Highly autonomous AI systems should be designed so that their goals and behaviors can be assured to align with human values throughout their operation.

11) Human Values: AI systems should be designed and operated so as to be compatible with ideals of human dignity, rights, freedoms, and cultural diversi-ty.

12) Personal Privacy: People should have the right to access, manage and control the data they generate, given AI systems' power to analyze and utilize that data.

13) Liberty and Privacy: The application of AI to personal data must not unrea-sonably curtail people's real or perceived liberty.

14) Shared Benefit: AI technologies should benefit and empower as many people as possible.

15) Shared Prosperity: The economic prosperity created by AI should be shared broadly, to benefit all of humanity.

16) Human Control: Humans should choose how and whether to delegate de-cisions to AI systems, to accomplish human-chosen objectives.

17) Non-subversion: The power conferred by control of highly advanced AI systems should respect and improve, rather than subvert, the social and civic processes on which the health of society depends.

18) AI Arms Race: An arms race in lethal autonomous weapons should be avoided.

Longer-term Issues

19) Capability Caution: There being no consensus, we should avoid strong assumptions regarding upper limits on future AI capabilities.

20) Importance: Advanced AI could represent a profound change in the history of life on Earth, and should be planned for and managed with commensurate care and resources.

21) Risks: Risks posed by AI systems, especially catastrophic or existential risks, must be subject to planning and mitigation efforts commensurate with their expected impact.

22) Recursive Self-Improvement: AI systems designed to recursively self-improve or self-replicate in a manner that could lead to rapidly increasing quality or quantity must be subject to strict safety and control measures.

23) Common Good: Superintelligence should only be developed in the service of widely shared ethical ideals, and for the benefit of all humanity rather than one state or organization.

Appendix 4

Table of AI Standards and Their Scope

Standard	Institute	Scope
ISO/IEC 2382-1:2015	ISO/IEC	Provides definitions and principles related to AI.
ISO/IEC 24027:2021	ISO/IEC	Establishes guidelines for AI governance, including risk management, ethics, and accountability.
ISO/IEC 38980:2020	ISO/IEC	Outlines requirements for AI-based software, such as safety, security, and performance.
ISO/IEC 42020:2021	ISO/IEC	Defines a framework for the governance of AI, covering topics like strategy, risk management, and ethics.
IEEE 7001	IEEE	Provides ethical considerations for the design and development of autonomous systems.
IEEE 7008	IEEE	Establishes a code of ethics for software engineers, including principles related to AI development.
IEEE 7009	IEEE	Defines a professional practice code of ethics for software engineers, with guidelines applicable to AI development.
NIST AI Risk Management Framework	NIST	Provides a framework for managing AI risks, including safety, security, and fairness.
NIST AI Safety Guidelines	NIST	Offers guidelines for ensuring the safety and reliability of AI systems.
ECMA 402	ECMA International	Defines a vocabulary for AI, including terms and concepts related to AI development and applications.

Appendix 5

AI Act at a glance

Aspect	Description
Main Objective	To regulate the development and use of artificial intelligence in the European Union, ensuring that it is safe, reliable, ethical, and respects fundamental rights.
Risk-Based Approach	Classifies AI systems based on the level of risk they pose, from minimal to high, and applies specific requirements to each category.
Unacceptable Risk Systems	Systems that manipulate human behavior in a manipulative way or exploit the vulnerabilities of specific groups are prohibited.
High-Risk Systems	Subject to strict requirements, such as conformity assessment, transparency, human oversight, and risk management. Examples: systems used in the judicial, biometric, and educational sectors.
Limited Risk Systems	Subject to transparency requirements to ensure that users are aware they are interacting with an AI system.
Minimal Risk Systems	Subject to minimal requirements but must still comply with the general principles of the regulation.
Fundamental Rights	The AI Act places fundamental human rights at the center, such as human dignity, non-discrimination, privacy, and data protection.
Transparency	AI systems must be designed to be transparent, allowing users to understand their decisions.
Human Oversight	The AI Act emphasizes the importance of human oversight in high-risk AI systems, to ensure that critical decisions are always made by humans.
Accountability	Providers and users of AI systems are responsible for complying with the regulation.
Governance	The AI Act establishes a European-level governance framework for overseeing the application of the regulation and for cooperation between Member States.

Bibliography

On Machine Learning

1. A. L. Samuel,. "Some studies in machine learning using the game of checkers". IBM Journal of Research and Development. 2000

2. C.M. Bishop, "Pattern Recognition And Machine Learning" Springer Nature, 2011

3. S. Russell, P. Norvig "Artificial Intelligence: A Modern Approach" Pearson, 2021

4. Yoav Goldberg, "Neural Network Methods for Natural Language Processing" Sprinkler Link, 2017

5. A. Vaswani, N. Shazeer, N.Parmar, J.Uszkoreit, L. Jones, A.N. Gomez, L.Kaiser, I. Polosukhin *"Attention Is All You Need"*, NeurIPS conference, 2017.

6. J. D. Hidary "Quantum Computing: An Applied Approach" Springer, 2021

7. Conference Paper "Quantum Computing's Path to Supremacy: Progress in the NISQ Epoch" Springer Link, 2024

8. A. Géron "Hands-On Machine Learning"with Scikit-Learn, Keras, and TensorFlow" O'Reilly Media, 2019

9. I. Goodfellow, Y. Bengio, A. Courville "Deep Learning" MIT Press, 2016

10. R. S. Sutton and Andrew G. Barto "Reinforcement Learning: An Introduction" MIT Press, 2018

11. A. Burkov "The Hundred-Page Machine Learning Book" Andriy Burkov (self-published) 2018

12. S. Raschka, V. Mirjalili "Python Machine Learning" Packt Publishing 2017

13. J. Howard and S. Gugger "Practical Deep Learning for Coders" O'Rollly Media, 2020

14. G.James, D. Witten, T. Hastie, R.ibshirani "An Introduction to Statistical Learning" Springer, 2013

Bibliography on Professions

15. A. Khang, V. A. Hajimahmud, A. Misra, E. Litvinova "Machine Vision and Industrial Robotics in Manufacturing: Approaches, Technologies, and Applications" CRC Press, 2024

16. H. Thompson, "How French tax officials are using AI to track fraud", The Connections, 2023

17. N. Basic "Tax audits using artificial intelligence in Italy" Fiscal Solutions, 2024

18. T. Wischmeyer, T. Rademacher "Regulating Artificial Intelligence" Springler Link eBook, 2020

19. S. Armstrong B. Mitchell *The Essential HR Handbook* New Page Books,US 2019

20. Chong Ho Yu, "Artificial Intelligence, Machine Learning, and Psychology" Oxford Bibliographies, 2023

21. T.H. Davenport, R. Ronanki "Artificial Intelligence for the Real World" Harvard Business Review, 2018

22. Ascarza et al."Retention Futility: Targeting High-Risk Customers Might Be Ineffective" Journal of Marketing Research, 2018

23. Goldman Sachs "AI is showing "very positive" signs of eventually boosting GDP and productivity" 2024

24. Pantano & Pizzi, 2020)."Artificial intelligence and the new forms of interaction: Who has the control when interacting with a chatbot?", Journal of Business Research, 2020

25. M. Field, " The DAO Handbook: A Guide to Decentralised Autonomous Organisations", 2021

26. International Energy Agency "Electricity 2024 Analysis and forecast to 2026", 2024

Bibliography on Ethics

27. P. Benanti "Oracoli. Tra algoretica e algocrazia" Luca Sassella, 2018
28. FLI, The Asilomar AI Principles https://futureoflife.org/open-letter/ai-principles/, 2017
29. S. Zuboff "The Age of Surveillance Capitalism" William Collins 2021
30. L. Floridi *Hypersuasion-* persuasive power and how to deal with it" Centre for Digital Ethics *2024*
31. N._Bostrom, " Superintelligence: Paths, dangers, strategies". Oxford University Press. (2014).
32. L. Floridi, "The Logic of Information: A Theory of Philosophy as Conceptual Design". Oxford University Press. (2019)
33. Jobin, A., Ienca, M., & Vayena, E.. The global landscape of AI ethics guidelines. Nature Machine Intelligence,(2019).
34. Taddeo, M., & Floridi, L. "How AI can be a force for good." Science,(2018)
35. Wallach, W., Allen, C., & Smit, I. "Machine morality: Bottom-up and top-down approaches for modelling human moral faculties". AI & Society,. (2011)
36. Whittlestone, J., Nyrup, R., Alexandrova, A., Dihal, K., Cave, S., & Calvo, R. A.. Ethical and societal implications of algorithms, data, and artificial intelligence: A roadmap for research. Science, (2019)
37. Paolo Benanti "Human in the loop. Decisioni umane e intelligenze artificiali, Mondadori Università, Milano, 2022
38. Paolo Benanti "La grande invenzione. Il linguaggio come tecnologia, dalle pitture rupestri al GPT-3, San Paolo, Cinisello Balsamo, 2021

ARTICLES OF REFERENCE

39. Topol, E. J. (2019). High-performance medicine: the convergence of human and artificial intelligence. Nature Medicine,.

40. Price, W. N. (2018). Ethics and artificial intelligence in health care. Journal of the American Medical Association,.

41. Kitchin, R. (2017). Thinking critically about and researching algorithms. Information, Communication & Society,

42. Terry, N. P., & Francis, L. P. (2017). Ensuring ethical use of artificial intelligence in healthcare: A prescription for success. Journal of the American Medical Informatics Association,

43. Paolo Benenati "Pacem in Cyberspace, Auspicia Algoretichs" in Ai in the Age of Cyber-Disorder. Actors, Trends, and Prospects, Fabio Rugge (edd.), ISPI-Brookings (Ledizioni LediPublishing), Milano, 2020,

44. Paolo Benanti *"Crisi della razionalità scientifica e paradigma tecnocratico"* in AA.VV. Profezia di Francesco. Traiettorie di un pontificato, EDB, Bologna,.

45. Wachter, S., & Mittelstadt, B. (2019). *"Why should we care about artificial intelligence ethics?."* The Lancet Digital Health,

46. Char, D. S., Shah, N. H., Magnus, D., *"Implementing Machine Learning in Health Care—Addressing Ethical Challenges."* New England Journal of Medicine, 2018

47. Margherita, A. (2022). *"Human resources analytics: A systematisation of research topics and directions for future research".* Human Resource Management Review,

48. Carole-Jean Wu et al. "Sustainable AI: Environmental Implications,, Challenges and Opportunities" Facebook AI

49. Hugo Touvron∗ e alt., "LLaMA: Open and Efficient Foundation Language Models", Meta AI corp.

50. Team PyTorch "PyTorch 2.0: Our next generation release that is faster, more Pythonic and Dynamic as ever" Meta AI corp.

51. OpenAI. (2022). *MuseNet: AI for music composition*.

52. Google Research. (2023). *MusicLM: Text-based music generation*.

53. Deloitte. (2021). *AI in Creative Industries: The Future of Art and Design*.

54. Microsoft. (2022). *Project Artemis: AI for player safety in online games*

55. Deloitte "Owning digital responsibility and ethics Future of risk in the digital era" https://www2.deloitte.com/us/en/pages/advisory/articles/digital-ethics.html, 2024

56. UNESCO Recommendation on the Ethics of Artificial Intelligence: https://www.unesco.org/en/artificial-intelligence/recommendation-ethics

www.ingramcontent.com/pod-product-compliance
Lightning Source LLC
Chambersburg PA
CBHW050528160726
48003CB00001B/499